Wings Of Rhapsody

A Dalliance Of Poems

Selected Poems

Seema K Jayaraman

Become
Shakespeare
.com

First published in 2016 by

BecomeShakespeare.com
Wordit Content Design & Editing Services Pvt Ltd
Newbridge Business Centre, C38/39,
Parinee Crescenzo Building, G Block,
Bandra Kurla Complex, Bandra East,
Mumbai 400 051, India
T: +91 8080226699

ISBN 978-93-52016-35-8

Contents

Contents

Contents

Contents

Contents

Contents

Contents

Foreword

Poetess Seema Jayaraman's book of poem Wings of Rhapsody - A Dalliance Of Poems is a timeless gem. Her insights and innermost thoughts reflects our own thoughts, thus her poem's have a universal appeal. She is a natural poet, poetry comes to her as refreshing winds from sunrise to sunset. It is amazing how she is able to insulate herself from her very hectic corporate life and personal responsibilities to capture rhythms of her heart in poetry, consistently. No wonder purity of her poems are not contaminated by the challenges of life that we all face.

She wrote her first poem at the age of twelve titled 'Time' saying:
"Time is just like a circle
Round and Round it goes
With neither beginning or an ending..."

No wonder her intelligent and questioning mind observed and absorbed things around her, which yielded this fine collection of timeless poems! Width of themes on which she writes her poems and the depth of sentiments expressed in each of her poems are breathtaking.

In her poem 'A Blazing Sun' she says
"A million rainbows
Winking kaleidoscopes
Suspended tiny globes
Beckoning into promise...."

Seema's command over English language and her ability to mould in as per the needs of her poems is commendable. No wonder each of her poems leaves a lasting impression on the reader. Seema's poems hints at her journey of self discovery as expressed in her poems. Experiencing life from an early age, seeped in rich cultural heritage of her family, constantly conversing in her poems as she navigates through her life, thus leaving delightful imprints of memories in her verses.

In her poem " Where Did you Go' she says
"Do you stand next to me
A brilliance invisible to me
Whispering laughter s in my mind..."

Reading her poems is like appreciating a painting with all its hues, vibrancy and grandeurs. In her poems she talks spontaneously to herself, talks to nature and to the universe.

Through her poem 'Powai lake' one can visualise -
"Mile long sheet of mirror laid,
Pale moon light waltzed with,
Strings of purple and gold..." in her words.

I believe that "we are not what we do for living, we all are bundle of talents waiting to bloom". Unlike any other hobby, poetry can not be called a hobby, you have to be a poet to receive the poems from the almighty's treasure house of poems. All we have to do is to tune in with the universal rhythm, and stay connected. In fact I find that a poets romance with poetry (muse) is a very tender and private affair.

Poetry is the vibration of the heart. Poems are always our original thoughts. Some seeds of thought germinate as poems. A good poem is indeed a seed for many more poems. Only a great poet like Seema can capture so lucidly life's happy or tragic moments (when our dear ones leaves us 'like a smoke'). She have the ability to stitch together layers and layers of memories of togetherness with your friends, like a garland of flower, fragrance of which wafts through poetic minds. Keep writing such wonderful verses.

Only when time is ripe a flower blooms, same is true about our talents and it's fragrance, even the tree is unaware of its potential blooms and the value of its fruits. My dear friend, tune in and receive the poems from oblivion. My Blessings are with you Seema.

In her Poem named 'Draft Poems', she says the same
'one day, some day, I will roll my poems in the oven of mind...'

Most remarkable achievement of Seema is that though living through the din and bustle of a mega city life like Mumbai, Seema's poems breath to life nature inspired muses, spreading fragrance of nature's beauty like a blossoming flower, filling the readers mind with introspective thoughts, delight and deep appreciation for mother nature and soothing frayed nerves.

Poetry is part of Seema's being, coming to life recently. I believe she is a natural and gifted poetess beginning to unravel and revel in her natural gift. Her introspections and writings have the hallmark of a great poet who visits earth once a few hundred years. I expect Seema to emerge as an outstanding poet of our time.

Sujit Kumar Mukherjee - Author, Poet and Technocrat
skm567@gmail.com
March, 2016
Member of: IWA - member International Writer s Association – USA
Poet Ambassador - India for World Body Of Poets
(PPDM www.poetasdelmundo.com)
United Poets Laureate International (USA) and

About Shri. Sujit Kumar Mukherjee

Sujit Mukherjee is a natural Poet, Author, a business leader and Technocrat. Widely travelled and highly erudite, his writings chronicles deep observations of nature, humanity, society and his own inner self. His poems have been translated into many foreign languages and are also in the curriculum of international school books. In India he was awarded the coveted best poet of the year 2013. He has written three books of poetry.

His book of poems Dewdrops was released by the President of India, Shri Pranab Mukerjee at the Rashtrapati Bhawan on 1st February, 2016.

He also had the privilege of meeting and presenting his first book of Poems - Dewdrops to former President of India, Dr. APJ Kalam, Scientist, Author, Poet, National Leader and a himself a highly venerated beloved son of India on 7th March, 2014.

Dedication

This book is dedicated to my little angels, sons Rajjath (9) and Rohit (5) for their love and patience belying their young age, indulging a Mummy returning late from work, who always seems to be a whirlwind, flying around, getting muddled in some adventure or the other and lately streaming poetry from her being

Not to forget my darling niece Rhea (10), New Jersey, USA who taught me the first rules of Haiku writing in 2015.

This voyage of self-discovery through poetry would not have been possible without the support of my loving parents – Jayaraman and Shakunthala. This first book is especially dedicated to my Mom, she being the central pillar of our beehive, making sure the family is fed, cared for and safe while I wandered around following my heart's calling seeking to materialize thoughts and emotions clamoring for release in the form of poetry.

Lastly to my loving life partner and ever patient companion my dear husband Raj, without his support and encouragement materializing my poems in a book form would not be possible.

Preface

Poetry is magic, the human psyche attempts to materialize for various reasons. Poems are magical verses, words strung together by the nimble mind of the poet, enticing and leading the readers through a momentary gap in reality and time, into another dimension. Painting with words, a place of wonder, joy and color, creating a range of emotions, the Poet through their introspections leaves the readers with insights, inspirations and motivations.

Poems are highly cathartic both for the creator giving an avenue of expressing all that is inside, all that is experienced and seen through the inner eyes, and for the reader opening up a door to potentialities. In the attempt to add that touch of wonder and discovery, the Poet uses all that is available from the tool box of vocabulary and grammar allowing the words to pirouette and emerge in light.

Introduction

In early September 2015, the world was brought to its knees with sorrow and anger at the image of a small baby washed up ashore by the Aegean Sea shore. Innocent victim of power, greed and fanaticism and the ongoing middle-east refugee crisis. Wiping tears, my pain and anguish at this terrible and futile tragedy refusing to subside, I found myself furiously scribbling, words emerged from deep inside. At first a few words, then a string of verses and finally a lengthy poem titled A Father's Grief.

It was like I was on auto writing, the tragedy gave me the impetus to grab words of protests pouring in from I believe universal consciousness. With a sense of awe I snatched these words from thin air and watched them take form. I was writing creatively especially poetry after a hiatus of nearly 20 years (I used to write in my school and college days).

Once my poetic muse re-found its voice, I started taking cues from visual, nature inspired and emotional triggers, from events occurring all around, as we rush through our mundane modern life. I prefer writing happy thoughts, my words are intended to fill the readers mind and heart with joy, serenity and a sense of appreciation for the myriad forms of nature, at times motivational hoping to bring about a positive change through introspections.

My writings are a glimpse of real dialogues between me and myself. Words keep bubbling and churning inside, they boomerang and ricochet in the inner chamber of my mind, till I catch each elusive one and send them flying on a neuron for a burial in space inside my brain. But there are times when feelings and emotions are stirred very deep and a few lines in the form of verses spill out, make my fingers write out the thoughts otherwise that wouldn't have seen the daylight.

I started seeking avenues for sharing my expressions with a larger audience and came across UK based Leavener's Poet's Corner. A digital platform, created and managed to showcase emerging, aspiring poets.To my delight I received a very encouraging and positive response from their Project Manager Ms. Jorine Beck and Chief Guest Curator Mr. Ciaran Hodgers, informing me that my submissions for December 2015 were selected. I was **chosen as the Showcased Poet of the month December 2015** for **Leavener's Poets Corner, UK.**

I felt the strong urge to gather my muse loosely scattered on various forums, in a book form. An anthology – of my best poems to be shared with a wider audience. An eclectic mix of various styles of poetry, this book is divided into two main sections. Part one has a collection of free verses, meter based regular styles and part two has the highly intricate Japanese styles of expressions in Haiku and Tanka Styles. This book is a presentation of my early experiments in poetry writing.

Recognitions:

- Showcased Poet of the Month December 2015 by Brimingham, UK based Leavener's Poet's Corner (www.leavenerspoetscorner.com).
- Listed in the Awesome Poetry Profiles by Performance Poets, UK (www.performancepoets.co.uk).
- My Poem - Why Blame Me A Blood Moon displayed at P Cafe Stirchley, Brimingham, UK (Feb 2016)
- My readings of Two of my Poems A Father's Grief and Why Blame Me A Blood Moon were chosen and hosted along with an International mix of accomplished poets on Audioboom by UK based Poetry Group 365 Scribble FB Private Radiopod. The Anchor Neil-Kinsey Fagan himself a highly acclaimed and recognized Poet and Artist. (Mar 2016)
- My reading of A Father's Grief - was also played on The World Comes To You - Private Radio by Poetry Motion group, UK hosted by Poet Alan Johnson (April 2016)
- My Poems: An Ode for a dear friend late Capt. Sumita Vijayan were played on Red Shift FM Radio, Mixcloud, UK hosted by Poetess Rebecca Cherrington (March to July 2016). The poems chosen and read were:
  - I will never say goodbye
  - My Friend
  - Salute

- Where did you go
- Me & My Amorous Moon
- Childhood Days
- Eternal Lust

- Nominated for Sanmati Best Poet 2016 Awards - Aagaman Group along with 10 other finalists (India, Dubai, USA). The results will be announced in October 2016.

- Featured on Sunday Gaurdian Live on 3rd July, 2016 (Print copy and soft copy) in article titled Poet of Small But Memorable Moments - as an upcoming poetess to look out for. The link is :http://www.sundayguardianlive.com/books/5524-poet-small-memorable-moments

- Poems played on private FM Channel and RadioPods: The World Comes To You By Poetry in Motion, UK, A Tryst With You In Sin and Let the Storm Rage Silently mixed with music available on YouTube and SoundCloud.

- Poems on Friendship available on YouTube, narrated by eminent voice artist and musician Hank Beukema, USA

- International Athologies including:

- Poets Against Inequality - Extended Edition by Poets Unite Worldwide (This Anthology of poems is listed in Amazon, for charity, Led by Dr. Fabrizio Frosini and Italian Physician who gathers poets around the world to write on topics highlighted by UN guidelines)

- 'By Land and By Sea' - For Refugees by Poets Unite Worldwide

- **'Songs of the Earth - An Anthology Of World Environment Day Poems' led by Dr. Ampat Koshy from The Significant League Group**

Part One

Inspirations from Nature

1. Why Blame Me, A Blood Moon

A magnificent 'Gandharva' wedding
Planned in the night sky
Sun, and Moon in groom's attire,
Earth bedecked as the Bride

Destiny wove in good humor,
A velvety dark blue tapestry
And built a celestial altar
Studded with bodies heavenly

Arrangements, centuries in making
Declared a rare sight,
With several luminaries, orchestrating
A visual spectacle bright

With autumn season chosen
The equinox for A 'Muharat'
Planned on a Sunday night
The day of harvest arrived

Seers and the priests, forecasting
As visionaries, bad omens it augurs
Predicting an impending apocalypse
Where none or Earth would survive

Down on earth Men of wise
Wrangled front seat invitations
To witness mysteries of nature
Unobscured in a clear sky

Moon being slight in demeanor,
To impress the discerning bride
Puffed his chest, to perigee
Crowned himself a new name – Super Moon

Sun knowing his vast stature and size
Arrogance over his might
Assumed the center of universe,
For the would be impressionable bride

A star spangled garland in hand,
Dame earth coyly at Sun, glanced
Then she swayed a wee bit closer
To the widely beaming Moon

As she closed the gap, earth so deeply shy,
On Moon's face, cast a deep red dye
Moon all with pride, did a crimson blush
Deep auburn in hue, Moon was all aflush

Earth made her choice,
That flaming romantic night
   with moon in offing a duet
And they came so close, as Moon bent low
To place a kiss on earth's brow

Sun showered blessings, the ever gallant knight
With the magic of the moment
Cast all colors of sunrise and sunset
In the light of a pyre, the marriage solemnized

The doomsayer's went on with their quibble
Waggled their fingers and proclaimed the dire

Blamed poor Moon a Blood Moon,

Earth beware, for the poor choice she made

They said the warm shade Moon's face, portends

Future wars, to be fought by your seeds

On your surface over ill-gotten gains

Will end in disastrous means

While the newlyweds, a moment of eternity

Consummated their togetherness in bliss

Such was a wedding that did happen

A story of love unrecognized by poor men

_____

(3 October, 2015) (1)

Note:

Based on the Lunar Eclipse of 1st October, 2015, during a full moon called Supermoon when Moon was the closest to Earth and appears especially bright and mysterious. The last and fourth in a series of tetrad in a period of two years. As the lunar eclipse developed, earth's shadow cast a deep rusty red color on the moon's face, which triggered this story in my mind. While many were busy finding hidden doomsday messages I was compelled to see a different romantic view - signaling in from the moon, which gives us hope for a happy healthy world.

This poem was selected and hosted on their premises by PCafe Stirchley a social poetry and coffee tête-à-tête site Birmingham,

UK in the month of February 2016 for their patrons to read, relax and enjoy. My reading of this poem was chosen and relayed with a host of international poets on Audioboom a private Radiopod by UK based facebook poetry group 365 Scribbles. The anchor is Neil-Kinsey Fagan himself a highly acclaimed poet and artist. (Mar 2016)

2. A Blazing Sun

I opened my eyes
To blazing sunlight
Streaming unchallenged
Flooding gold dust bright
Into my amethyst room

A million rainbows
Winking kaleidoscopes
Suspended tiny globes
Beckoning into a promise
Day of sunlit laughter

If only I was willing
To discard this dark shroud
Of gloom and despair
Covering my minds dishabille
If only I had the strength

To reach out to these orbs
Tiny twinkling rainbows
Spinning in and out, evanescence

Gather these ephemeral diamonds

For my minds unlit corners

_____

(25 January, 2016) (2)

3. A Firefly's Perspective

Wavering panes of light

Reflected on sleepy lakes face

Darkened cushion of water

Gently rocking huddle of boats

To clanging bells of a temple

Prepping the Gods for the night rest

By the discarded lights

Flickering from lone street lamps

On a deserted lake bank

Seen in the drop of a moment

Seeking a haven to rest

By the telescoping eyes

Of a firefly, desperately hurtling

Down the man-made bridge

Arching high over the lakes

Darkened yawning belly.

_____

(20 December, 2015) (3)

4. Late Night Song

It starts sharp ten, just as I am adrift
– the chickaree rhythm
Picking through the weaves of my dreams
A pair of jangling anklets,
Out on a clandestine errand
Beyond the shadowed arbor,
Of a gently fragrant garden

They jangle like a rather,
heavily woven silver links, intricately
Twined into design masterfully,
worn on delicate feet
At first I blamed the little creekers,
hidden under eaves
To them I tender my apology,
Now that I know better

I had my ears plastered,
To their every move and sway
Of the clanging made by the secret crusaders
So I lay and wondered,

Half asleep half perplexed, could it be a bird

Could it be calling its mate,

Or a squirrel scampering between trees

I hid and peeked through the gaps

Of my darkened curtains at wee hours

Thinking of surprising the culprits,

To nay, I snuggled into restless dreams

As the ankleted visitors,

Beings from other dimensions

I believed, hummed and piroutetted

their frenzy, to love's ballard

Under silver moon beams

_____

(4 November, 2015) (4)

5. Love Cry of Crickets

Tossing sleepless, to the knock out din

Pelting orchestra on my window screen

Sounding like a high pitched turbine

Revving of a supersonic animate machine

Bounding in pitch from high to higher

A crescendo of uncensored chorus

The two beat chant,one intermittent

Carried on still air, like a banshee wind

Teeth jarring in my clenched chin

With the dark nights ablaze

Reverberating to love cry of Crickets

_____

(2 November, 2015) (5)

6. Powai Lake - Mumbai's Pride

Still waters of a large lake
Miles long sheet of mirror laid
Pale moonlight waltzed with
Strings of purple and gold
From the yet far off breaking dawn

Down its length by its edge
Out on a salubrious pre-dawn ride
Mesmerized, shrouded misty wake
Mysteries hidden deep in its bowels
Mumbai's pride, freshwater Powai Lake

_____

(16 November, 2015) (6)

7.   Purple Blooms of October

Imps, Ladies demure and shy
In swatches 'ades royal purple
They snag my eyes and vie
An explosion in violet and mauve
Lavender, Lilac, Periwinkle dye

On my way, Starlets, star drops Orchid lay
Painted sparkles, Amethyst lace
Winding vines twirling pave my way
Mulberry Iris Periwinkle trace
Feathery plumes skirted all October day

Sprays of boysenberry, tiny raisins boast
Unimaginable shades of Magenta rage
An accidental sight raised to my toast
Coyly each floret covets my gaze
Garden of Sangria blooms afloat

_____

(13 October, 2015) (7)

8.   Drenched 'arth

Patter On Leaves
Wave high notes, wet mud
Inhale, October rain

Inky 'ark horizon
Patter tinder dry leaves
Swill drenched 'arth

_____

Mumbai (8)

9. October Drizzle

Under an inky dark canopy
I hear the rustling of leaves
A light patter, a little pitter
Uplifts a ruffling breeze
Stirring skirts of sleeping trees

A wave of light notes, heavenly
Wafts in and swells up, intoxicating
Announces the heady swill of -
Parched earth lightly drenched
By late October retreating rain

My heart exultates, thirsts for more
Oh for a downpour, a drowning
I' be a peacock unfurling iridescence
Dancing free, you will find carefree
In nature's nectar raining down on me

(11 October, 2015) (9)

Note:

Last night I heard the leaves rustle, next there was this heady intoxicating essence wafting up - parched earth lightly drenched by a light rain in October. The five minute drizzle was a welcome heady experience especially the indescribable, intoxicating heavenly perfume, parched earth sprinkled lightly by rain. Love that intoxicating heavenly smell which no man made perfume has been able to bottle.

10. Monsoon Fury In March!!!

A birthing sun stretched, outreach golden fingers
Over the arch of, pre-dawn's auburn wings
There was no hiding, the high octave of light
A sunny spring morning, a day in March bright

Gay and cheer unfolding,peeped under shut eyes
Calling the slumbering, to shift sleepy gears,arise
A grey veil crept,gossamer silk like at first
Unseen sweeping overclear blue skies, a crust

Around shimmering sun,climbing the high mound
In a lace of fluff, unheard the wisps wound
While that fine dawn, dressed an awakening choir

On a just lit fire, rendered apart watery womb,
Down burst the shower, as I watched from my pane
Lavishing a coppery fury, liquid gold raining
The power of thunder and rain on a parched mane

Weaving a monsoon magic, swept in a curtain of
    spray
Laced in the smell of earthiness of wet mud

On a happily swelling land, kneaded in sunshine

Pleasantly surprised that spring day

_____

(1 October, 2015) (10)

11. Dawn

The golden gleaming ball
Peered above the horizon
Embedded on her - sparkling jewels
She opened her eyes and
Kissed the sleeping world, a secret message in dreams

Lo and behold, morning breeze
Sweet and gay, so fresh it comes
Kissing all along the way
Her tender touch
A simple message - hard work and peace

The flowers swaying in rhythm
Nodding their heads, life is so gay
Dew drops winked and gleamed
Pearls dropped by magic from far off sea
And the farmers in the field, sang out the message

Green burgeoning boughs, bowed
Soft rustling leaves, laden with vigor
Fruits of labor, visible, hearty treats

Birds came chirping, fluster of busy bodies

Twisting and gyrating to the breeze

My heart missed a beat,

This visual paradise, laid out shimmering

Wooly clouds in azure blue sky

Green earth grounded with gold and brown

For my eyes to behold, this beautiful precious sight.

(1984) (11)

Note:

This is one of my earliest poems written at age of twelve. Written in my seventh grade in my school K V Koliwada (CGHS), Mumbai it made its way in to the School magazine that year. I remember walking with pride, a huge feather in my cap those days. I discovered the power of words, the power of English and how they could be arranged and rearranged to mesmerize. Decades later when I shared this poem with UK based Leavener's Poet's Corener, their Project manager Ms. Jorine Beck informed me that this Poem was one of the most popular ones with several enquiries from their followers.

12. Seattle Blossoms

As I spring from the community transit
Warm smiles and morning wishes, echoing
A deep breath and the view unfolding,
Of winding roads and far off buildings
On a rainy and cold late winters day

Feel my heart swell
Where sunshine plays hide and seek
with wet days
I revel this morning,
For I am a girl and I skip in the rain
There is the promise of the Sun yet to come
An important meeting and a presentation

Feel life surge, my feet springing on asphalt paths
Hiding in my hood from the gentle shower
Stepping over puddles in my high heel shoes
Walking tall, business suit and confidence for makeup
On my way to work lugging heavy laptop and notes

Seema K Jayaraman

I pause and ponder, he miracle

Of cherry blossoms budding

Bravely on winter withered bare trees,

A promise of pink on study of brown,

A million needles pointed skywards

Turning velvet, soaking in the cold rain,

Unfurling a live feed

The wink of an eye and my world

Blooms into a million shades of pink

At my feet, these unnamed flowers

threatening the rain

On long slender upturned brown limbs

With their upturned young buds ready to burst,

Chorus of cheer, yellow sunshine

The far off mountains as though in a painting

The budding trees, awakening earth and me

The promise of a magic about to begin

Layers and layers of soft light cascading, curtains

Tingling air, trailing nights cool melting

As I cross over the silently surging brook

On my way to office, the meetings in calendar

For leading management gurus and technical teams

Complex theories on presentation boards

Wine and dine, important luncheons,

To plan strategy and budgets

and to lead million dollar projects

Yet these verses at the start of a working day

Remembering my origins in a far of land,

Drawing 'kolams' on my Grandma's verandah

Her toothless smile and me clad in a saree on my

    knees

Sharing the heart of this stubborn impy girl

The one who left your warm shores

Urgent war room sessions,

hurriedly arranged in office lady›s room

The one who called on ISD"s

With rebellious tones and weepy voice

Continuing with the promise

Of a tomorrow and love to come

Burgeoning, loss of the familiar,

A new rainbow yet to appear

Laid bare, the turmoil,

My thoughts of you, life and nature

_____

(2004) (12)

Note:

This poem welled up one cold very wet early spring day in Seattle, USA. I was on my way to work, braving through a light drizzle thoughts about the work and assignments of the day in mind when the light pink buds of Cherry Blossoms tightly wrapped in dark maroon covers springing on bare tree limbs in millions caught my eye. Made me pause in my stride and gaze at their bravery in wonder and admiration for defiantly attempting to bud through the cold and wet season.[44]

Introspections and Earthly Bondages

1. A Father's Grief

As I held you in my arms, sinewy of all
The anchor, to hold you secure, eternally
Promises, A Father to his child, inscribes
Etched in their souls, spelled through the eyes
This crook, most solid and sound I sold

Forever here, the mast with you sheltered
I will stand aground, rooted,
So no harm dare stray near
No wind and no tide, no destiny could prise

To catch, console, when you stumble and stray,
A rough caress here,
A gruff lullaby for Baby whimpers
For you the harbor of my shoulders, I carved
To groom you in a better image,
My sail tattered I unfurled

Seema K Jayaraman

In the rocking ceaseless tossing,
Evil willfully designed
Banshee winds, towering seas,
Bloodied land left behind

Through waters that had beckoned,
the only routetTo freedom,
A passage to future bright,
Other avenues denied

When the ship's shepherd,
threw away the steer
Swindled again, deceived humanity,
The enormity of black scape

Wheels I held - the last fight,
your savior Me, to deliver
With only a prayer – Daddy Be Safe,
Upside down I realized

I felt you slip, surrendered,
the nightmare, that never should be
All I held dear, in that dark moment,
Snatched from me

Desperate souls in black night,
In darker depths, drowned in treachery,
Dreams asunder all perished onboard,
A destiny n'vr agreed

We were tricked, deceit craftily snitched, my life
My bubble, My froth, My fizz –
All I ever hoped to be
That moment, eternity merged
with Now and never, all denied

God welcomed his light,
Earth and humanity left bereft
Yet to this wild, all undeserving zombie – Men
A reminder, to heed, to heal and apologize

Look my brother,
the treacherous waters, did concede
a most delicate & tender shell,
that once held a cherub inside

That which mother of all mothers
Could not hold
From her dark churning depths,
she returned from her womb

Rocking on thundering waves,
So gently a shining pearl
Ashore a wet tear swept golden shore, she gave
Now to the arms of human race I forsake

Witness my baby, my babies fragile,
Nary a delicate hair askew,

Nor the clothes worn or shoes,
In place their angelic glow

For those with heart to weep,
Lesser beasts to repent
I carry the corpse of my being,
Weighed down by my empty shoulders

_____

(September, 2015) (13)

Note:

This poem welled up from deep inside in early September 2015, my personal homage to Mr. Kurdi and his family and to all families who are forced to live through war and strife and the loss of loved ones especially young children.

This poem is a mark of deep anguish on behalf of humanity, their pain and loss is beyond comprehension. Our beloved Earth is being turned into a gallery of destruction, death and evil reigns, in the name of religion, in the name of greed, in the name of intolerance, all in the end to gain control and power.

I wish there was more I could do and offer, all I do is offer you these frail words and my prayers. The intention of A Father's Grief is to provoke introspection which hopefully someday will bloom into a major mass movement for universal peace and acceptance for safety for small children. My reading of this poem was chosen and relayed with a host of international poets on Audioboom a private Radiopod by UK based facebook poetry group 365Scribbles. The anchor is Neil-Kinsey Fagan himself a highly acclaimed poet and artist. (Mar 2016)

2. All Trussed Up - Packaged for Delivery (Against Human Trafficking)

Wide eyed horror, why do you look at me
It definitely is, a human child in a cardboard
So here I am on your Facebook post
Pictured a forward, could have been lost
Like a chicken all trussed up,
Knees drawn high to chin
Arms tightly wrapped over shin
Brown duct taped, two tight spins
Teeny patch plastered over lips
To hold my screams of terror within

You appear aghast and mortified
Lifeless scrawny girl, kidnapped from poverty
Snatched from the labyrinth of humanity
You wonder what dividends ever justify
Barbarism scavenging off hapless vulnerability
Another victim marked for human slavery
So tightly bundled up, in pitch darkness I lay

Seema K Jayaraman

Not even air through my folded limbs

Life snuffed hurriedly, in my cloistered coffin

In vain, for release from my captors I prayed

You look at my south-eastern features

Glossy long bangs, bruised cheekbones

My tears stained face, hue pale

Don't bother fixing my nationality

Cause I could belong to all humanity

So many more like me regularly preyed

Brutally abused by every hand all day

It doesn't matter whether I died on the way

My organs could revive the rich near dead

Or as a sex slave or short lived cheap labour

Lifeless, you wonder why I died

An unclaimed package in a warehouse

What scared off the pickup guy?

A cop chase or a barcode crash

Or maybe a customs skirmish

That left me cold and shut eyed

Did I come through a ships folds?

Or flew in through an aircraft hold

I wish I could share those stories

Had they left me enough to breath

You wonder what I held close, in my terror

Sweet memories of lullaby in a loving home

Or last hours of torture by my bestial perpetrators

Was I from farmlands or Countryside's

Or from gutters bordering suburban shanties

Had I been blessed a roof and school roll

Was I picked playing on sidewalks

Or lost the hand of a well-heeled Mom

At a bustling city mall, it doesn't matter

What could a waif do seven or eight years old

You think aloud, how I could fit

In a brown box just two feet by three

Any child an accomplished contortionist

I could have demonstrated were I alive

And with hands that wrapped me tight

I assure you I could have fitted a smaller size

Blood clotted quickly, so tight my confines

You might have to break a few bones

Before you straighten my limbs

Stiffened at so many joints, in rigor mortis

You pray for a miracle, my picture never seen

So you don't have to labor a share or a pause

Cause I couldn't belong to your relatives

Age and sex no bar, neither the color of currency

A market for free labor, organ and slavery

An unforgiving wilderness around you exists

A depravity un-paralleled in this world

So my story untold, a mystery for cops to unfold

A prayer is all I seek, let no child be born on earth

To line greedy pockets that sacrifice innocent births

(28 October, 2015) (14)

Note:

This was an outcry against an unbelievable social crime against a small girl child. I came across a picture in my Facebook with a little girl in the frame probably seven or eight years old, with south-eastern features trussed up in brown tape, mouth sealed with tape, eyes shut tight with blood stains from nostrils being unwrapped by cops from a cardboard box. The little girl was dead but the cruelty in the picture left me speechless.

This is my protest, I hope more public awareness will bring a stop to this barbarism. I wish all governments would unite for this one cause **AGAINST HUMAN and CHILD TRAFFICKING**. My intention was to provoke some serious attention to this horrible crime, I hope more awareness and outcry will help in focusing public outrage against this heinous crime and put a stop to it worldwide.

3. Rape of Innocence / Ripped By Faith, I will survive

Ma, do you remember, you woke me up
A light caress on my forehead, a golden wish
Brimming love, your beautiful child in bed
For another day, a day in paradise
Or so you thought, my school would be

You fed me the best, cooing ancient stories
Of glory of our past, teachers held above God
The glass of milk, for my bones to strong,
You took pride in my healthy glow
My thick shining hair and twinkling eyes

Ma you bathed me, scrubbed me free of dirt
Dressed me up, in your hand washed uniform
You checked my notes, with me all sharpened
Homework in place, crayons all packed
You packed my food, three varieties full

Ma you carried me in, the ride on you lap
On our way to school, I was still your baby

Seema K Jayaraman

Just wee bit taller, me still suckling my thumb
You wiped my tears, through the gate
A small admonishment to behave

Ma, did you not see, the gates enclosed
With wrought wires, a place most dark and
    foreboding
Its tall dark trees encircled, shadowy dark beings
In its deep recess, evil eyes pried the little ones
Were many like me, its next innocent victim

Ma, at first I didn't know what it meant,
Emboldened, he thought he dared
Further misadventures, my body as a dough
Dirty and defiled, but you taught me obedience
When garnled hands, twisted my innards for mirth

Ma, I know, you didn't birth me for this,
You know nature didn't design my body for this
Early footsteps in corridors of learning, smudged
My safety inside the haloed premise in shambles
The venerated guru, a beast in guise

Ma, I a mere chit at the start of boyhood
You left me at the safest landings of learning's
Laughter filled classes, gardens and grounds
Little did anyone realize, these barbed walls
Encircled a pen and fed young ones for vicarious
    pleasures

Ma, my will bent like weed,
Under fierce commands of the highest custodian
To whispered ugliness, quaking I bade
And watched the stains, from my ripped insides
The haloed halls bowed in shame

Ma today as you weep, by my bed
As I swing between life and death
Today an entire city weeps, with you
They beat the gates, an institution vandalized
How many more need be victimized

Before the nation and world wakes up
I feel the shivers in spine, many Ma's fearing for
    safety
They go looking for ole dried blood stains on the wall

Look no more, those forlorn downtrodden eyes

Tell tales on the pyre of our innocence

_____

(28 October, 2015) (15)

Note:

In protest of a shocking and painful incident in a local school, a six year old little boy of 1st grade was allegedly raped by the Principal the school. I came across a huge mob of outraged parents and police outside the local school and couldn't believe this was happening in my locality (14th Sep, 2016). The child traumatized and hospitalized in serious condition and Principal absconding the whole city was reeling from shock. Words fail me, I cannot comprehend how the highest guardian of a school could fall to such bestiality. The highest, harshest and maximum level of punishment should be handed in such cases to act as a strong deterrent for evil to breed.

4. How Does It Feel

How does it feel Oh! My Heart
To be so unloved, not their part
Solitary in this bustling world
Why must you fend alone

They whom you called your own
They tread low, cast you down
Walk through, you don't exist
Why my heart this low wail persists

Mend your ties with loneliness
Its reign over your heart possess
The power inside of silence
Universal love to your presence

Lay all your hurts and despair
All this never did matter
Love a mere illusion
Let God's light be your reason

1993 (16)

5. Inequality - In You The Rich Thrive, Soul Denied

Convoluted Man's history, regale sagas of Inequality

disappeared mysteriously, coffers and sovereignty

A global allegiance, citizenship exclusive, two and

    sixty

Truth be told, the elite thrive, their franchises feed

    frenziedly

The poor, the fuel, the fodder, gluttons honed to

    depravity

Multinationals and their wealth supersede nations,

God easily found than their parent organizations

Stolen wealth of common man, shored up in foreign

    vaults

They devise Clever interludes, havens for Siphoned

    billions

A derisive dollar as tax, they snigger and appease

    conscience

Women and children, the lowest rung of victims

Under paid, sold for father's pyre, raped, she fills
    niches

Starving, naked in winter, her babies untended,
    she has dependents

In glass lined skyscrapers, on stiletto, she tip toes

Masquerading as ragpicker, through
    scraps of company revenues

Century of enlightenment, poverty stark, walks
    with glossy brands

Some are sold young, as slaves to pay their father's
    pyre

Others watch their father, kicked in testicles to early
    grave

In freezing winter in the capital city, children paraded
    naked

Little girls at busy metros twirl like monkeys numb in
    nudity

A father hugs bowed shoulders with blood
    drawn knuckles bared

His starving boys scrapping steel of a gleaming SUV

Seema K Jayaraman

Well heeled ants with shining manes and coats in
  skyscrapers
Scrawny scabbed fingers scratch carelessly tossed
  green notes
Entire families eek on roadsides scorched
  besides multi nationals

Colossal waste everywhere, water, food, energy
  downed in drain
While rest of the world scavenges for morsels in
  shanties and dustbins
The world bustles by, those who can cast down their
  eyes
Vaunt the courage, to hold the bull of inequality by
  the horns
to share with all equally, fulfilling necessities,
  bounties of mother earth

Whenever Inequality tilted scales, history sings
  defiant tales
Nineteenth century, In protest of tax on Breasts
Nangeli of Cherthala, offered on plantain her
  chopped breasts
Mahatma Gandhiji for the right to Salt, walked
  'Dandi' miles

To burn the diamond castle, 'Sati' of poor, a

    conflagration perhaps

Staggering a poor earth awaits, birth of an alchemist

    Einstein

With a magical formula, a Robinhood, snatch one

    percent's trillion

Were it not to come, to reformat this inequality, a time

    machine,

Send a curse, a pestilence on humanity to lay Man's

    seed barren,

Lest the rich, one day, roads they pave with poor flesh

    human

----

19 February 2016 (17)

Love, Passion and Loss

1. A Tryst With You, In Sin

I wish for that indescribable feeling
blowing a delicate pink over my skin
Goose bumps threatening a march
From tingling cheek all the way to shin
The awakening through my spine,
passions kundalini languorously uncoiling

As I imagine your shadowy presence
slipping in through moonbeams
Just behind the corner of my eyes
Ushering in another romantic interlude
You whisper curtains over a bold moon
The soft shuffle, sinking foam, crushed dreams on
  pillows

The thunderous clap of billowing clouds
Split apart shyness of a burgeoning heart

And I dream myself laced in your arms

You Wound so tightly in my gossamer gown

Clinging like shredded cotton strands to night beard

Wafting Sandal sweats our rosewood four poster

The silver rivulets like amorous rain

Channeling down dusty memory panes

Longings a finger nail down strong veins

A faint pulse throbbing like crashing waves

My love a hologram in enclosed ribcage

With you a tryst, to soak and sink myself slowly in sin

----

1 March 2016 (18)

2. Jilted

To feel your warm fuzziness
Wrapped all around me
To wind myself like raw silk
The cocoon of your larval form

I snoop tattered memories
When sloshed sky high
And remember the heat
Of your strong embrace

Secret rendezvous many dusk's
Beneath our favourite giant tree
In the encircled park, your shoulders
Cozily cradled on my lap

When all we could see inches away
Moon and stars in each other's eyes
The soft rustle of your breath
Blowing crimson on my cheeks

Firing the flames of hot passion

Carousing lividly bursting hearts

Drumming fingers unbuttoned a rhythm

To tongues frolicking in passion

Whence we scratched eternal love

On brown weather tattered barks

I see the scars from vantage sight

As I pass by in wizened day light

Someday before I close my eyes

You need to tell me why, Oh why

Did you have to leave like smoke

Blown clean by a callous breeze

Do you from your new space in life

Look back with heavily bleeding heart

With bitter bile of betrayal on lips

Regret love you left so soullessly jilted

(4 Mar 2016) (19)

3. Dance With Me Bare Feet

A wild tango, Hip to hip

Bodies swirling in soft light

On dawn kissed patch of green

The whiff of wet earth kneaded

By our curling toes, the paint of

Dew drenched velvet grass

Swing me to high heavens

Riding the rainbow stream

Your palms firmly in mine

_____

(15 December, 2015) (20)

4. Let The Storm Rage – Silently

You say you saw through the pretense

The calm demeanor belied the storm

Churning raging deep inside

The depths tumbled and plumbed

The restraints barely surface held

But, how would you know, the difference

You could be in the eye of the storm

The calm a mere mirage,

The storm whistling all around

The shift of the eye, you be snared

Topsyturvy thrown up in the air

While passions pound turf inside out

So trust me let the storm be as is

Deep inside, lest it surge and submerge

The reign of calm on the surface

(18 November, 2015) (21)

5. The glint in your eyes

The glint in your eyes
They speak a thousand words
In unheard languages
I am yet to comprehend
Or atleast allow me my pretense

So what is it you will have
A joy de tour on springy boards
Hastily in out of bound outskirts
Battled passion beneath pristine white
For the cleaning stewardess to find

Or the dance in silence
Where I am waltzed against walls
By invisible hands in caress
Love tumbled and awash
Still held upright by your eyes

Will it be the war of words
When the tongues all they want
to explode in a tango the lavish

The lust felt wrapped as love

While we debate on rights and wrongs

So tell me how would it be

All laid out as business pleasantries

As we conclude profound debates

Not a word heard or registered

The only take away the glint

An undying lament in sheathed eyes.

_____

(17 November, 2015) (22)

6.   Broken Heart

A stillness so vast, so somber

Like a blooming garden

Frozen in sudden autumn sheen

All the splendor and grandeur

Like a ghost from bygone years

Visions of carefree laughter

Seen through misting eyes

This mournful howl

To rekindle that one moment

Suspended in vacuum of time

Still held closely in broken heart

_____

(1993) (23)

7. My Loneliness

A Stillness so vast so somber
Like a Marigold shrub in
Its autumn shrug
All the splendor and laughter
Of the bygone years
Visions of carefree gay dancing
Seen through bleary cataract eyes

This is mourning for that
One glorious ride
Suspended in a vacuum our time
Enshrined in this moaning heart
A small capsule of your smile
The grey fog today seeks to hide
The radiance of bygone times

_____

(1990) (24)

8. Reminiscence

I have laughed so much
Till every spring, brook and river
Gurgled, churned and roared
Joining me in my joy

I have hurt so much
Till the whole universe
Vibrated and shuddered
Racked in my pain

I have agonized so much
Till my curled crumbling body
Rose howling into the winds
Dispersed in Saharan deserts

I have moaned so much
Till every breath I took
Was an avalanche in Everest
Throwing up shredded Ice

Now all that pain

A faint remembrance of past

Whence the girl, poured out

All the hurt, lost in path of love

_____

(23 January, 2006) (25)

9. All Engulfing Palm

Grasping the warm strong
All engulfing palm
Scrambling up the path
Of a boulder filled hill
Lit beneath the ochre
Of the settling sun
Shying from the wait
In the ever patient eyes

In the outskirts of a
Dimly lit suburb
With only a dilapadated
Crumbling shrine atop
Marking the passing away
Of eons, when once
Every few centuries
We clambered uphill

Not knowing whether to run
Downhill or continue holding
The palms pulling uphill

To the promise of magic

To be spun in the embrace

Underneath a velvety evening

Unraveling sparkling stars

Shooting in dilated pupils

_____

(23 January, 2006) (26)

10.   Loneliness

A lonely path in life they tread
Pair of eyes that beseech
For that one special sight
For that one and only sound
Your voice my melody
I seek in a chorus
Eyes till scanning hopefully
Your silhouette, endless sea
Scrapping my sighs from
Where it gives company
To my heart sitting in a chasm
I bundle my unexpressed need
Oh life is a sour mead
I left behind yellow memories
Of things that could have been
A hundred births,
The same dreams unfulfilled
In earth's light, Man never gleans
All that cannot be !!!

_____

(1993) (27)

11. Chasm Of Silence

And yet this unexplainable distance
The roar of this deafening silence
Sudden chasm that widens and separates
The gnawing in my heart unexpressed
What must I do my love to come closer
How wish a ropeway heart to heart bridge
As this Everest of yearning silently grows
And yet the chasm of silence widens on

_____

(1993) (28)

12.   Catch Me, I My Fall

Catch me in my fall

Soothe me in my despair

I cling to you in body and soul

Swearing my hearts allegiance

Oh this thrill

To experience this joy with a

Vengeance! !

—————————————————

(2015) (29)

13. Her Sorrow

Her sweet melodious hymn
Ringing from a heavy heart
Another pathetic tune
Woefully rang about her loss

Tears of pain pour from My eyes
The pain in tandem with hers
Her sighs echo in mine
My heart a river in flood
For is it mine or hers, love lost

Sometimes I still hear her
Moaning by the stream
Weeping her heart out
For what could not be
Deep inside I know her loss is mine

_____

(1988-89) (30)

14. Will You Be There Sone

When desolateness & loneliness sweeps
And my shoulders bend in defeat
Lift my spirits and give some solace
To bleed this bitterness and weep

Will you be there Sone,
When the world deafens in its crescendo
And there is no one to hear me speak
Lend your thoughts and hear my silence
To tame this wildly beating breast

Will you be there Sone,
When over rough rock strewn paths
I twist my steps and stumble
Cushion my fall and wipe my hurts
To place run away tendrils

Will you be there Sone,
When we realize our lives is a past
Days through which we laughed and lived
Share the burden of memories

To dry my tears and hold my sighs

Will you be there Sone,

When all alone, I quake and tremble

Afraid of sinister ministrations

You open arms to my haven for escape

Gently quieten my heaving heart

To a blissful slumber

_____

(1992) (31)

15.   My Ultimate Cove

Through murky waters I wade
It beckons, in a lonely haze
A silhouetted island, craigy and steep
The strange truth grips, hastens

Finally, as I kneel bedraggled
Dripping a pool of joyous tears
Facing confusions this distance
An empty chasm that separates

Oh why this awaiting stillness
Explain this pregnant silence
When just the last steps remain
Chains of time had inhibited

The explosion as glances meet
Eons of search in which we seek
A twinkle that flutters and glows
In tremulous arms we float

As I nestle against thudding heart

This rhythm, so familiar,

The ultimate crescendo, yes I know

My beloved, I've reached my ultimate cove.

_____

(October 1993) (32)

Frail Prints of Tender Emotions

1.   New Year

A delicate goblet fine

Memories, dredges of Red wine

Twelve months, of squeezed life's stain

Sugar and salt, days of joys and pain

With heavy feelings I reminisce

All my losses, sudden demise

Loved ones no more, at their sides

Just in time, for my last goodbyes

Gratitude, I remember trying times

Days lined, Wayward silver blessings

Recognitions unexpected, small victories

Sneaked help, friendly glances and murmurs

These closing moments, as you coast
I raise high my hand, one final toast
To drain last drops, effervescence you boast
Thank you for boarding, being a good host

I hope the new year arrives, happy tidings
Goblet of life's joy and riches brimming
Showering on this berthen, heavenly blessings
Good health, prosperity, peace and serenity

_____

(31 December, 2015) (33)

2. Fair Lady

Oh my fair lady

Fairest of all

Sunshine burst

Gold in milk white

Stir in rose petals

Delicate pink

Glint of saffron

Ochre high flags

Frail veins plum purple

Yet so virgin white

God made you at leisure

Gifted like his light

_____

(19 November, 2015) (34)

3.   When Ole Friends Meet

When 'chuddy' buddies meet
It's like quarter century unelapsed
Spanning the breadth of lives and earth
Like yesterday's high school pass outs
Never mind the bellies or scant pate
Through Veils of time and memories
Easily we reverted to those carefree days
Volumes spoken in grins and cheers
All churned and learnt in the last bench
So many reminiscences bantered
That small window of our meeting
Standing one legged with Bent knees
Romance books under skirts canopy
Questing young minds in Chemistry lab
Boyz scoring a brilliant pink
Precipitation experiments covertly with urine! !
Teen distrust, enmity of boyz and girls
Dissected frogs and live toads in 'tiffins'
We sized each other with fist fights and cuffs
And then ceased with truce for joint mischief
Furious games of volley balls and doze balls

Seema K Jayaraman

With intentions to smash wrists and shins

Western dance in the new computer lab

With teachers trying to figure mechanics

Of operating the damned shiny machines

Cassettes hidden in nests in exhaust fans

Oh those were the days of humble living

Tiffin 'dabbas' shared tasty morsels for each

Like fluffy butter our teachers churned us

Hopefully today we are better beings

But we still like the 'khattachaas' (sour buttermilk)

Spiced with life's chillies and curry leaves

―――――――――――――――――

(4 January, 2016) (35)

4. My Baby

The flush of cream and pink

Faint surge surfing tender face

Oh! So soft like the cotton seed

Floating released from ensconced cover

Your eyelashes curled over rising cheeks

Brush the color of early sunshine

Your puckered pink lips

The way they make a lopsided O

Blowing tiny bubbles ephemeral

When I hold and cuddle you

The sigh and coo and gurgle

That emanates deep within you

Is all the reward I need

To keep myself awake night on night

Watching every moment fall and rise

The gently drumming rhythm

The wonder of your soft eyes

Bond of several past lives

In the twinkle in your eyes

The way you turn your head

Slightly around to my movement

And to my sound, I am amazed

Always seeking your Mother's eyes

Your tiny little dimpled arms

The delicate pink of frail fingers

So dainty and yet so sure and strong

When they curved my fingers knowingly

I remember the first time

Trembling I tried a small manicure

With tears coursing down eyes

Imagining the pain when you flinched

Your perfect little toes a soft mauve

The numerous times I placed them

Over my eyes and face

Thanking God for the blessings

You brought home to me

I love you so, I tremble at the wonder

The right to call you as mine

So perfect God's miniature image

Placed in my lap to love lavish

The millionth time I caressed

Simply to reassure myself

That this was real you were here

To thank you for birthing

The Mom in Me!!

_____

(23 May, 2007) (36)

5. Life ~ A Sparkling Red Wine

I spin like a merry go round

Eyes closed, my joy knows no bound

Cart wheeling freely I'll be found

Sliding down slippery green mound

Holding aloft to the dawn jocund

Life brimming sparkling red wine

Spark incremented, eternal amaranthine

To carousels around campfires incline

Vixen's hot blood scalding weak spine

Dancing light foot I am a delicate glass stein

Color carousing my veins a deep burgundy

Caught criss-crossing thresholds of insobriety

Snatch from me you can't my sherry

Rendezvous on my cheeks stained ruby

Under rose arbor, bare limbs played rugby

_____

(2 November, 2015) (37)

6.   Purest Form Of Love

White doves in the sky
Endless, formless white of light
Apron that encircles

Present in form and thought
Womb offered later Arms to embrace
Mother, chaperone for life

———————————————

(2015) (38)

7. Mummy Aaj Chutti Hai!!

Mummy aaj chutti hai bolo haan aaj chutti hai
Abhi tho Shanivaar aur Ravivaar, kewal do hi din
Ghar par Aap sangh manaye hain
Aaj Somvaar, sapthah ka phela din, chuttike de do
nathum
Khel Khel thak, mein chaar saal ka, thodi sustha
loonga

Beta, abhitho do din gharpe hi manayen hai
Aaj Somvaar ka phela din, chutti na mana sakenge
hum

Mummy aaj chutti hai, bus ek din ki bolo thum
Dekho suraj ki savere laali, Mangal vaar ka yeh din
shubh
Pooja paat, katha aur lori, jabh tere sangh sikhoonga
School chodo, gharpe sari padayai, phir kyon yeh
atyachaar
Bus aajek din, tere godh mein, sarr mera sehlana tum

Beta, bus aajke din school ko jaana thum

School ka phone nalagta, chutti na dela payenge hum

Mummy chutti hai bhai chutti hai, bol bol

Aap ke kanhon ko masali, Budhwaar adbudh bada

Hariyaali aur bhagiyani mein, bhaya sangh keloonga

Aaj teacher se bolo, nanha mera na aayega

Thodi cartoon, thodi coloring, sofa par thodi si japki

Bus beta, aaj phir kitabonko dene ka din

Teacher ko apni kal waali homework aur nayi copy le

    lena

Mummy, bolo aur kitne din chutti ko nakarogi

Bus mein na jaaonga, aaj hai Guruvaar ko chutti,

    thum bolo haar

Naani ki godhi mein hota, mein chota sa umar chaar

Hote sukhein aur jukhein hain kandhe,

    phir wohi paat kyon baarbaar

School mausi mera na sunthi, aur baakhi

    doston ke jhulum haazaar

Beta, Mummy teri aaj badi so chein hain

kewal ek din aaj jana, phir kal sochoongi ek naya
    bahana

Mummy, sapthaha ka aakri din, mera bachpan na
    chino thum

bhari aawaz, ghele ghaal, ganga jalkhathi is
    Shukravaarko

Pathar dil, thum kyon na pehchaanti, van uncle ko
    phone lagaaoo

Bolo naajukh munna mera kamjhor pada, aaj naa
    ayega

Aur jhi bhar mein gale laaga kar, mamta barsaaongi

Vaise bhi weekend ke, do din phir se hain aaye

Mein bus chahoon, aankh micholi naani ke aanchal
    saar

Woh khil-khilana, aur besudh bateen keval bhayaa
    samajega

Har pal Diwali aur holi,Mummy ka bhar poor pyaar
    dulaar

Papa ke kandhoon par kite flying, aur naana sangh
    shyaam ko park

Somvaar ka ek din, teacher se

hateli par theen stars lene jaoonga

Bhaki ke pure chaar din ghar phar hi manaunga mein

(10 Septeber, 2015) (39)

Note:

This poem is for my little one, all of four, who sings this refrain without fail everyday not wanting to go to his nursery school. He says 'Mummy aajchuttihai' consistently, woefully, repetitively and with the maximum range of inflections in so many variant ways that our hearts simply melts to his pleas for a holiday. We rake our brains topersuade him to school with various carrots and bribes but the next day he repeats the same lines without fail. God bless him always.

8. A Delicate Drape

The day after you were delivered
As you lay all pink & bundled
Warm in the Cradle of my arms
Self-congratulating, smug, I lay

In wonder, watching that naughty Golden light
Flitting and brushing, the lightest touch
O'er curled strands, Oh so delicate
Brown trailing to invisible light

Tender curved, my breath, I held
Lest they rearrange, disturb your tryst with angels
A small tuft, the frailest of cluster
So well draped, so finely drawn

O'er the most perfect creation, God ever made
Huge brown pools of love
Beginning to stir, tiny sparks alight
A fleeting glint, at the brim of a new life

Few more days, I watched mesmerized

The whisper of brown, more strongly etched

Now a darker brown, trailing to light

Yet stubborn they continue to hide

The early realm of our first sweet memories

 A simple truth never can be denied

Nestled together, awakening in the mirror of our soul

The strength of this bond, that you are mine, you are

   mine.

(April 2007) (40)

Winged Wonders

1. Dawn's Litany

Patter delicate feet, padding lightly

Amongst crimson saucers erupts

Righteous riots spontaneously

Disrespect to dawns peace, bursts

Winged foragers squabbling brazenly

Hauled from slumber land abruptly

Barely over headboard, extended nape

Prise open a lash disobedient, flagrantly

Popping one pupil, unfocussed gape

Ensuing tree top bar brawl blatantly

Cursing hidden raven, crowing nosily

Unfocussed eyes surprise pair of robins

Madly arbitrating chores domestically

Hopping o'er delicate blossom crimsony

Crested napes banner scarlet unapologetically

Lashes as they rolled down, hauled rudely

Atop the highest scarlet tulip crown

Working curved hookbills furiously

A squawking majestic Jade, unyielding frown

Into the trodden blossom blaring ominously

Sighing loss of dreams, settling dormancy

Drawing from a full headed cluster

Holds a feebly trilling aural litany

Lovebirds, gesticulating in full fluster

Lashes fully opened by sounds heavenly

_____

(5 November, 2015) (41)

2. Rude Awakening

Bouncing in nets of sleep

Carousing winky waves -

Gently, I lay

Grasping dreams grey

In a Castle built on clouds

- shattered my slumber

Rude awakening indeed

Squabbling flock of Jade

_____

(5 November, 2015) (42)

3. Indian Bulbul On African Tulip Tree

Onslaught of sound - loud blows

Street side brawl I chanced

A black hooded squared knight

Cloaked in speckled chestnut gown

Spotted alterations Black and Brown

With a swab of red beneath angry trail

A visibly infuriated Indian Bulbul

Perched on highest farthest stretch

On Curved crab clasps walnut florets

Yet to unfurl and snare ochre of sunrise

Recipient of Unrequited ministrations,

Ire on feathers, raining taloned punches

Busily hammering the tender buds

To borrow the revealed crimson color

For a dash of scarlet o'r whiskered crown

And for a bow o'r its hooded cape

Continued to pulverize bowie basket

To squeeze the yet of tomorrow's red

Seema K Jayaraman

From a defiantly withdrawn mute buds

Tulip tree and I helplessly stood by

_____

(10 December, 2015) (43)

4.   Penguin

Podgy pelvic parade

Prancing propped up paunch

Prattling pompous pique

Podgy peculiar pout-

Penguin

(15 December, 2015) (44)

5.   Parrots

Sea of malachite high above
Sporting a bobbing grandeur
Striking emerald shrieking aloud
Parrots paddling African Tulip Tree

Beds of crimson starlet saucers
Sets of six or seven scarlet whorls
Some dreaming, some in half blooms
Sun soaking sirens hosting Popinjays

Blade the senses, spliced green
Pepper the tongue, crackling silly
A sweetened soda drink mixed chilies
Bursting flight of gregarious jade

_____

(12 October, 2015) (45)

6. Splintered

Regale me underneath

Blanketed by your ego, sheath'd

Blood moon prophesied, a wreath

Shine thr'u I'll, a million fireflies

Splintered glass earth, revealed belies

Emerge in Sunshine, one day, butterflies

_____

(26 September, 2015) (46)

Me and My Lone African Tulip Tree

1. Me and My African Tulip Tree

Sunlight toddling hide n seek

Netted high above in canopy

Waving waxy winsome weaves

Speckled sheets upturned leaves

Shades a million malachite green

Chanced upon a full basket

Crimson scarlet ochre blooms

Dreamily slumbering Tulip florets

Me and my African Tulip Tree

———————————————

(8 December, 2015) (47)

2. Crimson O'er Concrete

Carpet crimson untrammeled blooms

Crochet of velvet o'r paved concrete

Weeps lone city bred African Tulip Tree

_____

(December 2015) (48)

3. Shredded Tulip Bud

Shower of scarlet

Shrads of scorned spathe

Shredded - Tulip bud

_____

(13 December, 2015) (49)

4. Scarlet Shudders

Languorously floating down

The limb of a sun ray

Path of a curvaceous waist

Scarlet shudders taint

A discarded bloom, dreamily

On her way to grace

Warm concrete embrace

Me and my lone Tulip tree

_____

(8 December, 2015) (50)

Ode to Unsung Lady Warrior - Salute to My Dear Friend

1. Salute to my Dear Friend

My friend It hurts,

your silent au revoir

Purged by Jet fuel fire

White intense light un-seared

Blessed soul so light

Lady of deep blue skies

Unblemished friendship we sowed

In youth, far in our past

Took deep roots, emotional

Growing warmth intense

Coursing bonds of lasting kinship

Through our twined hearts

So when destiny without notice
Winged your soul to higher domains
It came with the wrench
The ripping of a million bolts
Attachments strongly held

My gasp, ripples from my heart
Like a never ending earthquake
Scoring a million on the Ritcher
Pulling away invisible energy - physical
I felt the love chains Stretched taut,
Then break

Into infinity the crushing weight
On my breasts
Like thousands of elephants trampling
My devastated chest
Like the tidal wave sweeping
Over my mind's golden beach
Gone my narrow stretch of sanity

In the ocean of despair and loss !
You know, I will hold on
The ripped chords - fiercely

As it cuts into my veins

Till my last throbbing blood drop

Like our wild friendship

We defended all these years

You know, no matter this fate

You will trawl in my dreams

Whispering wild adventures

Yet to be chased

Destiny's child, I will never let go

I will stand here and Salute you

My friend, the bravest of them all

Our hero, lady with silver wings

The one who soared the endless skies

I will never say goodbye

_____

(19 November, 2015) (51)

2. My Friend

I remember our gang jousting's
Growing up as pranky teenagers
One such debate on our heights
Contest for the tallest amongst us

And you remarked, one day
You would overshoot boundary lines
Be the tallest amongst us all
You would touch the skies

These words of yours I treasure
I cherish and roll in my mind
Whenever fondly I remember
Our happy carefree days of youth

You made your promises good
Went to soar the skies
Pioneer in so many fronts
First 'Malayalee' female Air Force pilot

So prophetic were your words

As though future seen and said

You set standards for us

Ordinary middle class girls

Your actions achieved glories

Many of us just wished and dreamt

You are the mistress of silver wings

Queen of all that soars up in skies

Today you choose to fly higher

Far off into the wide blue skies

But for these cords held in my heart

To tether you strongly in our lives

'Sumi', no matter where you go

No matter, from life to death

Today filled with disbelief and sadness

I declare, I will never say goodbye

(23 November, 2015) (52)

3. I'll Never Say Goodbye

I'm afraid to close my eyes tonight,

Lest I lose my grip on today,

Which held you and me alive,

Albeit in different parts

Of the world, connected

By hearts, cords of love

By invisible threads of

Unconscious thoughts, as long

As you and I breathed now

It didn't matter how far we met last

Knowing you choose to soar

Up in the blue skies,

Filled me with pride

Playing hide n seek always

With your friends was

Your favorite game

The most notorious,

Tomboy elite in our gang

Lady pilot, queen of blue skies

Mistress of silver wings

You played the same chance

Seema K Jayaraman

With life and death

As you flew in those

Treacherous terrains

It's not yet time to say goodbye,

You know I will never say goodbye

No matter how far your choose to fly

_____

(23 November, 2015) (53)

Note:

The above Poems are written in memory of my childhood friend late Capt. SumitaVijayan (Retd. IAF Officer). She became an iconic female achiever and torch bearer for women of our country. Selected and inducted into Indian Air Force as a lady helicopter pilot in the early batch of Women in the defense services, she had many firsts - was the first Woman Helicopter Pilot From Kerala.

Along the years she garnered several awards and achievements rendering numerable services to the nation, both while she was in uniform and post retirement. She always chose a low profile steering away away from media, instead her work and her passion for flying spoke miles high in the sky. She passed away on Nov 23, 2015 when the chopper she was piloting crashed in Katra, Jammu Kashmir. In coming years, her name will be added to the legendary hall of Hero's of Modern India.

Diving Into Time & Dimensions

1. Connecting With Aum

As I feel my way

Around in darkness

Floating weightless

Above and below

Feeling for the seams

A single thread to unravel

The portal of many doors

I seek suspended

The single cell of a

Multi celled honeycomb

An inlet imploding into infinity

or an outlet exploding into eternity

Knowing not I spin

Should I delve inwards

Should I explore outwards

Is it light my Guru I seek

Or my all pervasive Shiva

stretching into eternal darkness

I know not I know not

In abeyance my penance

I know not how or why

Teetering on the brim of a

profound discovery

All I do is I think I sense

Indrawn breath suspended

The stardust caught in moats

Floating under drawn eyelids

That connects me to the hummm

Of the living breathing Aum

———————————————

(2 March, 2016) (54)

2. Where Did You Go

Into light framed rectangular
Through portals manifold of white heat
Stacked layers of dimensions
Galloping through universes
Where did you go, my friend

Compressed a billion fold
Like a tiny dust moat
Master lady with silver wings
Name the universes now you float
Allow me to follow your trail light

Do you stand next to me
A brilliance invisible to me
Whispering laughter's in my mind
And I wade through hazy memories
Holding feelings tethered kinship

Whisked to higher realms need I find
A wormhole to book my flight

Zipping through fluorescent tubes

Into compressed microscopic domains

Will I find you o'r higher missions

_____

(5 December, 2015) (55)

3.   Womb, Suspended Time

Seeking desperately, Time

I paused to inhale deeply

Standing still, I found

Lit softly, A universe

In the gap, between now and then

A womb, suspended time

_____

(27 January, 2016) (56)

4. An Unknown Life

The warm friendly hand
Embracing and encircling you
As the peaceful eternal sleep
Come drifting on you

You enjoy the fine feeling
An angelic smile bedecks you
As your head slides besides
And calmness confronts you

Something so sublime, you never knew
These spectacular dazzling lights
Greet you to eternal life
From millions of glowing stars

Taken on this grand tour
Where destiny merges with time
Millions of universes away
Known only as dark death to mankind!!

_____

(1986 or 87) (57)

5. Time

Time's just like a circle
Round & round it goes
With neither a beginning or an ending
Bound on bound it goes
Never pausing for a bit of doze
Time is just a circle.

Spinning and spinning around
Making men sink down in it
With neither a beginning or an ending
Tarry a break for miles
Or a creak for a while
Time is just...

With glowing and blowing zones
It's got the worst part
For soothing the best parts too
Time is just a waiting
To reach the glorious shine

The celestial zone of peace

Where man can never reach

Swirling along the breach

The ultimate zone of peace

_____

(1983) (58)

Note:

Written as a 12 year old in my seventh or eighth grade, the era of library books as the only accessory for creativity...I must have written this in 1983 or 84, pardon the errors and simplicity, but a poetess was definitely hiding inside.

6. My Only Star

Gazing up at the inky sky
The mysteries it seeks to hide
I search for my only Star
A brilliance amidst lesser lights

Convey this knowledge, a simple truth
A beacon strives, strides and rides
Through the darkest tunnel
The call to life

Something shapeless, formless, imagined
So tangible, so visible so realized
Felling barriers, times and dimensions
Present, incarnated breath infused

Wing my thoughts, my dreams, my sighs
Yonder the abyss, the chasm of guise
Oh but only to bridge, to reach, to submerge
This song, a crescendo, convulsing me asunder.

_____

(1991) (59)

Limericks

1. Day After Big Run

Protesting purple

Blasphemy eloquently

Day after the big run

Wildly raging red

Bunion on big toe

_____

(18 January, 2015) (60)

2. Edge of Precipice

At the edge of the precipice

Wondering the depth of fall

Closed to the silent crowd

The family outcast, ponders

About to free fall into the Abyss

The Traffic signal turns green

_____

(15 January, 2016) (61)

3. Right, Turn away from the Mirror

Right, turn away from the mirror

Throw away from the person

Who holds you the mirror

Virtuality is cozier than reality

_____

(12 January, 2016) (62)

4.   God's Hammer of Justice

Just when we forget

Gods justice hammer fells

heavenly quells

Earthquake swallows,

Truant egos up whole

Earthly thrones wallows

Emptiness reigns

_____

(7 January, 2016) (63)

5.   Bitterness

Taste of bitterness

When you are a leftover –

In life's dustbin

Devoured sumptuous extravaganza

Sucked dry, bone marrow

By once called kith and kin

_____

(2 January, 2016) (64)

6. Practice Run

I planned to Run and set the trail on fire
In my mind I jogged, the tracks shook
In reality my body resisted and I crawled
Every bit of me protested, shook and quaked!

_____

(10 January, 2016) (65)

7. These Days, I like to be an Ostrich

These days, I like to be an Ostrich

My head buried deep in dirt, deep way deep

I will not, nay I will not,

Look up, lest I catch some One's eyes

I will not let the cat out of the bag

I say surely so, Let the sleeping Dogs lie

I need to not know, hear or say

All that happens must be natures design

There is a proverbial method to my madness

Dare I not speak of what I see, nor show the mirror

When I admire my emperor strutting about

So he doesn't have his robes, who am I to tell

Lest once again with my big nose

I get caught between doors, and once again

With ridicule and ostracization

Snigger and sneer, great fanfare indeed, I

Find myself, thrown outside the threshold

That barely have I got my toes, inside the door

As I drape myself on the very verge

Of large highly polished ovals, I am brain dead

Easily can I scuttle and cower for my bread

When wise counsels of experienced men

Wear wool over their eyes, me blind like them

Table set for rosy tidings, veracity never verified

A Far cry the flunkey's will describe

The lion roars, ensnared its might by rats

Precarious the house of cards

In a pack of cards, the joker am I

To cut a long story short, this writing I thank,

It's a blessing in disguise

_____

(10 January, 2016) (66)

Motivational Writings

1.   Can You, Can You

Can you, Can you,

Maintain this pace

All it takes

Is a will like steel

The mind on goal, fixed

Let your body

Roar and launch

Shed the minds load,

Break the chains,

Merge like light

With wind matter less

See yourself

Fly and soar

With Mind focused,

Direction in compass set

To where they will flows,

Arms and limbs will follow

Muscles and blood in unison

Propel you on course

Being one among,

Eager straining millions

When the clock shouts start

Keep going, sweat rolling

Being there,

Breathing that air

Is all that matters

Scream of muscles, drowned

In enthusiastic shrieks,

Keep on going

The crunch of bones, lost

As Bodies jostle,

Let nothing stop,

Nourished by exhilaration,

Feet kiss timing pads,

Each milestone crossed

Bend the curves,

Strain the uphill's

Chorus your ears, the win

Can you, Can you

Kiss the red laser ribbon

Thoughts unloaded, only image

See self-sprawled on finish line

———————————————

(18 November, 2015) (67)

2.   The Wind On My Face

The feel of wind on my face
It barrels down on me
As I struggle with my pace
Trotting the gentle slope
Call my feet on turf to prance

The wind created by my race
While not a strand stirs, breeze dead
Today as I work to keep my place
The upcoming SCMM marathon
International juggernaut relay

I thank the sudden wind
The gust uplifting, my collapsing sail
Sound of my bones, as they bend
The wrench of muscles as they tear
All made worthwhile by this wind

Greeted thus, wind kissed cheeks
Cool ministrations on heat laced

Seema K Jayaraman

My companion in labored rounds

Cheer and freshness I taste

This breaking dawn, as I race

_____

(18 November, 2015) (68)

3. Mumbai Marathon SCMM Jan 17, 2016

Today Mumbai's bosom will resonate

Harmonious symphony

Of thousands of sneakered feet

Pounding the asphalt

True spirit of free Run SCMM

(17 January, 2015) (69)

Note:

I participated and completed my second major half marathon in an internationally recognized and highly prestigious Marathon event – Mumbai Marathon 2016 (SCMM 2016)...and improved my timing too. This run is dedicated to my friend late Capt. SumitaVijayan (Retd. IAF officer).

Pangs of Birthing A Poem

1.　The Gasp Of A Poem

The fluster of feathered fingers

Beating loudly weathered wings

An olive chickaree's rustle

Taking off all in a fluster

Trailing my harkening heart

My head, filled with fuzzy warmth

Words heedless – gasp of a poem

About to launch on fledgling flight

_____

(16 December, 2015) (70)

2. A Poem Is Born

Words drum a rising tempo
Synchronized, a million nerve endings
Pulsate, abuzz like a beehive disturbed

In tepid waves lapping the river bank
Awaiting release of water upstream - a roar
Announces an incoming tsunami - a poem is born.

_____

(21 September, 2015) (71)

3. Draft Poems

For now I serve
My deep emotions
"Piping hot" unseasoned
Fresh off my hot head

Lest my light scrawls,
Thoughts ephemeral
On sands of mind
Scrawled, be erased

One day, someday
I will pick and hold
Each etching of mine
Vaulted on PH

Roll them around
In the oven of mind
File and polish
Each word and rhyme

Till they glow
"Kohinoor" in shine
For enthralled audience
To admire and quote

Until that day arrives
As greedy treasure hunter
I stretch my fingers
To grab each rough one

As they boil and emerge
Rough crystals untumbled
From universal conscience
Lest they vanish to nothingness

_____

(19 November, 2015) (72)

4. Cooking a Morning Poem

I hemmed and wrecked my head
To remember and write out a recipe
To pen the perfect set of words - poetry
Toasting each dawn - a tasty savory

Rightful phrases minced and diced
Tossed vaguely remembered feelings
Deep fried in intense emotions
Layered mix of verbs and rhymes

All that time consuming baking
With mostly absent ingredients
I gave a large roundabout
Instead settled a quick scramble

A fluffy light lay of words
Spicy at times soothing garnished
Imagery - healthy dish of simple poem
I began to serve each day

(5 November, 2015) (73)

5. Embers of Creativity

Besides the grey fireplace
Of a cold desolate house
Sitting on the cold stone
At the foot of the bare hearth
On a tattered bent shoulders

Seeking writings inside closed eyes
Long killed in realms of physicality
Materialize Fire embers in brain
Stoking a thought to 'Boson'
Seemingly random act of creativity

To spell out the self-locked inside
A stray spark flies, to light
Looking to kindle a flare inside
Stir a bonfire within vaults
Of long emptied Imagination

To writhe out an inferno so profound
Move mountains, combust chains
And build a frenzy, a conflagration

Seema K Jayaraman

Just about a flickering candle
Next to the heart's inferno

A history of repressed holocaust
In every wake of modern life
Truth remained in eyes, un-penned
Sputtering life, in absence of Oxygen
Elusive 'Neutrinos', freedom of right

The embers dying, leaving grey coals
Wheeze and whine, inside wintry shrine
Empty altar rung with hollow bells
Give up this scintillating thought
To scorching speech, honest rhymes

Give in, lay down, and acquiesce
Hang on to chores mundanely
The genius anyways, long murdered
As snowflakes drift down the chimney
Extinguishing, the spark, long gone

Now all that is left, a tinder gone cold
Grey and white ashes resembling coal

Perhaps this burnt out coal

Someday in some fireplace, will

Enflame an incandescence of spirituality

_____

(11 October, 2015) (74)

6. The Birthing of A Poem

These sounds hum and ricochet
Somewhere deep within my brain
Elusive like breeze on fingers wet
Trailing outside windows of a train

Whimsical they have me enslaved
Triggered by a fleeting memory
Sight or sound, inane or profound
Life strummed up, a melody

Bleary my inner eye, scanned my mind
To give this buzz a form a name
Ephemeral, they materialize and dissolved
Like salt, in mid-summer rain

They pop my head, in explosive light
Gun shots in enclosed space, fanfare imagery
My eyes recognize, no sunrise nor sunset
Till the thoughts emerge, in disarray

Laid besides my pillow, a sprinkle of words

Putty to be plied, cornered on paper

Late night scribbles, strung to perfection

Emerge in daylight as gems bright - A Poem

———————————————

(29 September, 2015) (75)

7. The Accidental Poet

With many a friend steering mid age crisis
Future deeply thought, planned and dissected
To avoid mental arthritis, well laid out devices
Some adopted new age forums, promptly derided
Majority plodded on, nine to nine on clock's

A few bent ol'e musical wires, to capture
Others were honing rusty vocal chords
For audiences hapless in imagined rapture
A sprinkle plucked away, French and Spanish boards
Raising hefty slogans, practicing hasty departures

A lucky few choose to drown in drinks
Setting off exotic trips, surfing sun kissed beaches
Spiced up days with empty drags, lopsided grins
While a few choose to remain proclaimed dinks
Envied raking their nails, up foreign cliffs and craigs

Here left to myself, pondering my future abyss
Rapidly I unwound many a discarded scheme
Seeking holy grail, immortality, silver lined pockets

Engraved for posterity, basking in imagined fame
To preserve golden name, I engaged in mind games

Knocked and rummaged, every nook of my cranium
Tossing many a nights, plundered many a dream
Wrinkled on my pillow, dredged from my depths
A litter of scribbling, doodled of invisible ink
I found orphaned words, my nocturnal ranting

Deciphering outpourings, daylight reality
Laid out for the world, a modern art of words
Strung together for the sense, prose too miserly
I agreed to rearrange the words, a canvas of poems
Thus was born a poetess - albeit so accidentally

_____

(29 September, 2015) (76)

8.   Poet In Exile

Miserable, wallowing in self-pity

I while my few moments of silence

Watching the city lights whisk by

Marveling at the pangs, reclined

Want of a pen, some paper

Or the more familiar keyboard

All for the paucity self-defined

A twenty four hour day bound

Eighteen waking hours unwind

Chasing life's wants and demands

Six hours to sleep consigned

The writer inside, in exile

Living a life of self-denial

Helpless stands by, watching

Tides of thoughts ebb and flow

Erased the faint scrawls

Scratched on sands of mind

———————————————————

(17 November, 2015) (77)

Introspections and Lost Meanderings

1. Whirlpools of Anger

A whirlpool of anger

Whorls inside outside

Universe swinging out of control

Pivots on promises empty n naught

Spins venom spit on earth

_____

(24 January, 2016) (78)

2. Private 'Thaandavam'

Now I've lost it and slipped
Earth pulled from beneath
Forced to transform my calm
Let me rage in my own

Private 'Thaandavam'
Across multi dimensions
Striding fire thru multi-verse
Grind this pain to stardust
To lay it finely evenly
Falling through to my
Present realization the reasons
To wrap myself in semblance
Of sanity lighting the darkness
The energy of furious dance
Will drum into my conscience
The rhythm of normalcy
As we know it now and here

_____

(24 January, 2016) (79)

3.   Silent Screams

In the shattered silence

Your deafened ears

Won't hear my screams

I'm a walled up rejection

Battling demons you raised in me

_____

(2 January, 2016) (80)

4. Things Left Unsaid

So much left unsaid

Burgeoning, to break free

For today I did some talking

With my sneakered feet

Pounding out the tarmac

I spelt some out

In a crowd of runners

Unheard in the cacophony

Thoughts aloud I dribbled

I withheld the ending inside

For another rendezvous

When with sneakered feet

Midst a wave of runners

I can sneak my thoughts

Aloud on cold unyielding tarmac

To be trampled on by strangers.

_____

(3 January, 2016) (81)

5. Indian Bride –
Caught In A Traffic

Scattering rectangular

Lights on concrete in twilight

Reflects a heavily decked

Pensive Indian bride

Being rushed to meet her fate

Caught in traffic snarl

———————————————

(20 December, 2015) (82)

6. Accused

A niggle, astir, unbearable to the soul

The wrong done, unspoken

Surrounded, I stand

A wall, People I care, stare

Fingers pointed, whispers ringing

Frown lit faces, eyes unmet

To hear my wails, not an ear lent

Woe buried, untendered hands

Bend they will, someday

Realize the fiction, hearsay

When not a word true,

So late, someday, they labeled me a shrew

_____

(19 September, 2015) (83)

Part Two: Japanese Styles

(Tanka, Haiku, Senryu and Haibun)

A.   Collection of Tanka

1.   Masculine Kerchief

Wafting you

my secreted diary

wrapped in your

masculine kerchief

dust tattered with age

_____

(28 January, 2016) (84)

2.   Salty Sea Breeze

Rounding the bend

of a sine curved sealink

assault salty breeze

cul de sac freed

tangy sea mistiness

_____

(13 January, 2016) (85)

3.   Seagull Flew By Sealink

White Sea arrow

shearing morn ash sky

silent rush of wings

flew by steel wire bridge

feathered symphony - lone seagull

_____

(13 January, 2016) (86)

4. Birthing Sun

Orange And yellow

smudged in purple mauve

nature birthing sun

five year olds pallet

blotched canvas painting

_____

(8 January, 2016) (87)

5.   Smoldering -

Half drawn blinds

unveil molten gold

smouldering dusk

dream of rough hands

hauling a satin waist

_____

(January 2016) (88)

6. Pearly Droplets

Pearly droplets

perch on curved lashes

orphaned words

of a bludgeoned heart

veil a departing sun

_____

(January 2016) (89)

7. Dawn Tickled Green

Dawn tickled green

glistening diamond drops

dew my thoughts

I scramble to gather

as they rise as mist

_____

(5 January, 2016) (90)

8. Flamingoes

Receding waters

wetlands crackle pink

flamingo's congress

grand ball of nature

carousel fiery phoneix

_____

(4 January, 2016) (91)

9. Dew Drops

Dawn tickled green

glistening diamond drops

dew my thoughts

I scramble to gather

as they rise as mist

_____

(5 January, 2016) (92)

10.   Grey Fog

Murky grey fog

merged morning sea

fluttering flags

tugging tiny boats

disappear into horizon

_____

(5 January, 2016) (93)

11. Carols Flustered Gulls

Bridge over bay

marsh of white specks

surge snowflakes

natures feathered bounty

carols flustered gulls

_____

(24 December, 2015) (94)

12. Boats In Twilight

Twilight mauve casts

arrow array five boats

clanging temple bells

rocked from deep reverie

precarious clinging lovers

———————————————

(21 December, 2015) (95)

13.   Love Cry of Crickets

Sleepless dusk
ringing knock out din
high whine rusty engine
crescendo of my thoughts
reverberating love cry

_____

(13 January, 2016) (96)

14. Salty Sea Breeze

Rounding the bend

of a sine curved sea link

assault salty breeze

cul de sac freed

tangy sea mistiness

_____

(13 January, 2016) (97)

15.   Flaming Tangerine

Muted Dusk of

flaming tangerine

lavish sunset

mauve clouds quilt

orange scarves frill

_____

(4 January, 2016) (98)

Collection of Haiku

An attempt to capture Haiku in (2-3-2) Syllable Meter

1.   Oranda Gold Fish

Ochre

ornament -

orandas! ! !

_____

(5 November, 2015) (99)

2. Buried I

Buried

sense of I

pay emi

_____

(4 October, 2015) (100)

3. Poems!!

Saved

few ole gems

poems!!

_____

(7 October, 2015) (101)

4. Freedom

Bondage

rip 'ains,

freedom!!

_____

(7 October, 2015) (102)

An attempt to capture Haiku (5-7-5) Syllable

Dawn / Sun Rise

1. Struggle

Bruised horizon

signs of cosmic struggle

a birthing sun

_____

(7 January, 2016) (103)

Sunset/ Dusk

2.   Lavish Sunset

Muted dusk

flaming tangerine

lavish sunset

_____

(4 January, 2016) (104)

Moon

3. Struggle

Burgeoning Moon
shedding sheets of silver
blushes like the sea

_____

(6 February, 2016) (105)

Birds

4.   Seagull - Haiku

Silent groan

sliced dawns horizon

gull's vertical dive

_____

(15 January, 2016) (106)

5.   Sea Gulls - Haiku

Undulating bay
fog crested waves
cry of sea gulls

_____

(24 December, 2015) (107)

6. Winter Ducks

Silvery ripples

surface v shaped

winter wet ducks

_____

(18 January, 2016) (108)

7. Wakening Sunbird

High green canopy
fluster in bowie basket
wakening sunbird

_____

(13 December, 2015) (109)

8. Sparrows @ Sunrise

Twittering sunrise

nesting high windows

sparrow chicks

_____

(5 October, 2015) (110)

9. Sparrows disappearing from Cities

Radiation kills

cell towers city sky

sparrows rarely

(5 October, 2015) (111)

Note:

Delighted to see Sparrows flying in on my windowsills past few weeks. Never realized the once so common tiny birds would disappear from the city skies without a noise and without anyone realizing they were gone. The blame is falling on city mobile towers, the radiations from these towers seem to be driving these small brids away.

Flowers

10.   Fragile Petals of Rose

Luscious Red

fragile petals of rose

paint lascivious lust

_____

(7 February, 2016) (112)

11.   Heady Jasmine

Inky dusky sky

pearly white stars vie

heavenly jasmine

(6 October, 2015) (113)

Note:

Remembering the heady notes of jasmine blooming in the courtyard at dusk at my grannys home

12.   Swatches of Purple

Swatches of Purple

scratch corner of eyes

october blooms

_____

(13 October, 2015) (114)

13. 'Rajinigandha' (Tuberose) – Haiku

rajinigandha

thriving bouquet, memories

heart notes at dusk

(5 October, 2015) (115)

Note:

Haiku as gift for my darling hubby on his b'day today. Remembering the huge bouquet of Rajinigandha (Tuberose (Polianthestuberosa) flowers with which he had intoxicated me in a superfast train years ago.

Rainbows

14. Million Rainbows

Sunrise drum windows

dancing through crystal chimes

few million rainbows

_____

(November, 2015) (116)

Fishes

15. Starving Gold

Fiery Explosions

agitated aqua crimson

-starving goldfish

_____

(5 November, 2015) (117)

16. Orandas (Goldfish)

Orange Oriental

organza ornamental

owlish -orandas!

_____

(5 November, 2015) (118)

Others

17. Dozen Butterflies

Dusk at summer

dust storm warnings

dozens butterflies

_____

(12 December, 2015) (119)

18. Ocean Of Light

Ocean of Light

horizon fog disperse

laps lone boat

_____

(3 December, 2015) (120)

19. Larval Cocoon

Spun sap silk

dishabille now embraced

embosomed – cocoon

———————————————

(18 November, 2015) (121)

20. Granite Mountains

Looming blocks lay
majestically jagged grey
curtains of – granite

_____

(16 November, 2015) (122)

An attempt to capture Senryu

21. Pensive Wait

Pensive wait

reprieve of elderly wife

strangers at door

_____

(27 January, 2016) (123)

22. Evening Traffic - Senryu

Sea flickering red

on downtown road

rear lights to home

_____

(7 January, 2016) (124)

23. 'Nimitham' – A Sign (Senryu)

Son at school

image of smiling goddess

calm mom's nerves

_____

(17 December, 2015) (125)

24.   Memories

Memories flight

friend no au revoir?

twangs - luv cords

_____

(3 December, 2015) (126)

25.   Mars (Haiku / Senryu)

Red Orb spin in sky

man on earth mesmerized

explore "mangalyaan"

_____

(7 October, 2015) (127)

Crafting a Haibun

1.   My Friend's Waist

A fluorescent hoopla ring unattended on the floor. Few seconds ago it was merrily swinging away on a tiny waist. Brought memories decades old another tiny waist, my best friends. We used to hold and swing around and round. The universe swinging in step with our merriment.

Slender ring

fulcrum to swing round

my friends waist

_____

(13 December,2015) (128)

2. Awakening Sun Bird

Standing next to the black metal grille, half asleep tracing the play of Dawn's first light battling its way through shades of waxy leaves. A sudden fluster, in a basket of crimson Bowie Tulip florescence. A wakening sunbird stretching its tiny wings from inside its bed of curved chestnut tulip Floweret.

High green canopy

fluster in bowie basket

wakening sunbird

———————————————

(13 December,2015) (129)

Acknowledgement

This is my first book of poems in which I have stitched together my loosely scratched poems. As an aspiring poetess and a novice in the world of literary and creative writing, these poems are collated for ease of reference and simple reading by my small set of dedicated and enthusiastic supporters, family and friends.

My book would be incomplete without remembering my teachers from KendriyaVidayala's that I journey through early and high school especially Mrs. Usha Shukla and Mrs. Mitali Rudra from K V Koliwada, Mumbai (CGHS) guiding me in my Poetic discoveries.

My sister Pinky (Seena Sharad, USA) and a clutch of relations and cousins – for those wonderful childhood adventures running wild in the countryside of Kannur (Cannanore) during our summer vacs especially Sharmi (Sharmila Bhargavan), Shyna (ShynaHemant) Salma (Salma Pradeep), Danny (Daneshattan), Money (Santosh), Vidya (Vidya Bhargavan), Anoop and Sanoop. I trace the roots of deep appreciation for nature coming from the sun and rain soaked in Kannur life.

My Ma-In-Law Uma Mohan for her support and blessings and my Sis-in-law RoopaVarma for her editorial contributions. The early reference and inspirations to write from my uncle Mr. Aneish Kumar, a highly accomplished corporate leader, writer and artist - heading a multi-national Bank with whom I used to share my writings by post during my school days. My biggest fans and a very indulgent Uncle & Aunt (in laws) Sunderappan & Geeta aunty.

A long list of friends indulging my creative madness especially Purni (Purnima Santhakumar), Vishi (Vaishnavi Ramakrishnan), Manoja (Manoja Acharya), Minu (Minoo Mullins Patel), Seema (Seema Achan), Sumi (late Capt. Sumita Vijayan) and Yogi (Yogesh Kapoor).

Remembering the source of this guiding light coming from my grandparents, their indulgent chuckle as I emerged from yet another adventure, my Achami (late Kallakandy Narayani), Achachan (Late P. Gopalan Master), Ammama (Late Srimati Gopalan) and My Moothappan (Late K. Sreedharan).

About The Author

Photograph: Seema K Jayaraman

I think of myself as a pirouetting spirit, a global citizen having absorbed into my being a range of cultures over the years. This book of Poems is a journey of self-discovery.

I juggle multiple roles in my present life, fighting for space and time to fit in my routine the chaotic creative thoughts churning constantly in my mind. Thoughts which at times emerge as words and rhymes popping up unexpectedly catching me unawares. I am a full time working Mom, mother of two little boys, a Banking IT professional with over two decades dedicated to Professional career.

A resident of Mumbai, India, my roots are from the ancient land of "Naura" now known as Kannur (Cannanore), Malabar region of Kerala. Kannur the land of lores and looms is also called the 'Crown of Kerala'. State of Kerala is known as Gods

Own Country and verily so. Kannur is a mystical land, with a liberal sprinkling of many temples large and small, small 'kavus' shrines open to nature and nature worships, and a range of ancient tribal art and dance forms. The most famous being the colorful enacted prayer performance and storytelling - 'Theyyam festivals' ritualistic dancing to the beat of drums held in each temple for several days and weeks witnessing which has kindled my esoteric interests in nature and spirituality.

Being around and reading/discussing about crystals, mountains, flowers, higher dimensions, space travels, temples and mythology are my key areas of interest and my channel for finding my inner space and self. My free time, I get by bursting into more frenzied activities which is mainly travelling, visiting places soaking in nature. My friends and family tell me, they love me for my energy, undying quest to visit and travel and then share these experiences.

I did my post-graduation in Science and over the years have acquired a few additional degrees in Management and Information Technology subjects to assist my job functions. These days my vocabulary usage is limited to professional and IT related discussions, writing technical notes and presentations.

The seeds for Poetry and poetry appreciation were sown in my early childhood, with the practice of reciting daily prayers and Hindu shlokas supervised and encouraged by my grandparents. Especially so during our visits to Kannur during long summer holidays, gathering with cousins in the evenings around the fully lit 'Vellaku' (Diya) and reciting our prayers with the elders correcting the pronunciations and emphasizing the rhythmic sing song delivery of prayers.

Later by my teachers of KendriyaVidyalayas, constantly encouraging my participation in poetry recitation competitions in multiple languages English, Hindi and Sanskrit. I began writing Poetry in my seventh grade a few of them made their way into School magazines. However eventually life caught up and my writings became sporadic thanks to long working hours and other demands.

Growing up as an Airforce child, I have travelled extensively within India absorbing India's myriad hues and cultures. Over the years thanks to my IT career, I gained exposures to varied experiences, cultures and cuisines at both domestic and international locations mainly in USA travelling from East to West based on Company and project requirements.

The good side of it, I thoroughly enjoyed travelling the beautiful expanse of UA countryside, the majestic mountains and the wide plains. Experiencing snow, climbing mountains laden with snow, climbing the glacier of Mount Rainier were some of my most cherished and exhilarating experiences being a tropics born and bred Indian girl.

The trigger for embarking on poetry as a means of expression restarted last year in September 2015 with the images of the little baby boy washed up ashore the Aegean sea. Since then I find myself scribbling away, at times like someone possessed mostly writing my thoughts out on my cell as I commute or late at nights after my kids have gone to bed. I felt the need to expand my horizons and share my muse with a wider set of audience and hence the idea of putting them together in the form of poetry book emerged.

'My poems are expressions of wonder, an appreciation of nature in her myriad colors and forms and motivational introspections on human and nature events occurring around us silently which we typically tend to miss in our self absorbed fast lives.' - Seema

Contact:

Email: Seemakj@yahoo.com
Twitter: @seemakj24

Pages and Blogs:
https://en-gb.facebook.com/seema.jayaraman.1
Facebook Group: Mystic Verses
https://www.facebook.com/groups/953475531415211/

Facebook Page: Breaking Free - Poems https://www.
facebook.com/Breaking-Free-Poems-1525189397811952/
www.poemhunter.com/Seema Jayaraman
www.facebook/breaking free poems
www.facebook/flights to freedom poems

Testimonials

Excerpts of testimonials on the Poems showcased in this book, mostly taken from an international mix of poets and writers who have reviewed these Poems and generously added their learnt comments.

1. General

Ciaran Hodgers, UK – 'Seema writes with a naturalistic, lyrical style that is both engaging and surprising. Her work on the page begs to be read aloud, which is atestament on how carefully crafted and accessible her imagination is. I enjoyed reading these poems, which was more like listening – they played out in my mind full of sound and senses. Her work hearkens to a romantic tradition, drawing on landscape and nature but her craft is a contemporary one'.

Dr. Trupti Jayin, Mumbai - "Seema's poems are thought-provoking, they churn you up with lucid images and strong emotions. They appear to create a story on your imaginary celluloid and draw you in with their sincerity. They strike a chord in you, as many of them resonate with loss, mayhem and personal tragedy. A book of poems which heals. I loved it." Keep writing.....and healing...Love, Dr Trupti Jayin (Clinical psychologist, occupational therapist, Past life Regression therapist and founder of SETU, Gestalt therapist, NLP trainer, EMDR facilitator, Art and Creative writing in past life exploration, Key anchor of popular TV show 'Raaz Pichle Janam Ka')

Mana (Soul Science) (Mar 2016) - Seema's poems are like photographs in words capturing a time and a place, a space, and a frame of mind. One can open the book to any page for a feeling of true human history, which includes emotion, events, and states of mind which have touched us all." lots of love and best wishes for the book!, -Mana (Spiritual healer, popular author of Facebook Blog: Soul and Books 11:11 Time for Abundance and Soul Songs)

John Kavangah (UK) (Mar 2016) Seema, a poet / poetess like you only come around every 100 years or more, this is your star, it has been planned that now is your time even before your birth, I have read many many poets work and by the fifth line I have had to put it away because it made no sense to me, but yours has everything within, Heart, Soul, sadness, hpe, fortune and misfortune, and more, Your work is inspiring, comforting etc, read the comment by Mark Walker on my Poetry page, get the feel of what you offer to people by your hand and mind, believe in yourself because so many already believe in you now, blessings my dear Seema.

Oh my dear friend, reading so far into your poetry, you no longer are budding you are blossoming, Your words, descriptions, structure, and the way you engage the reader is among the best, and I mean that with my heart and soul. I don't think you know deep down exactly what it is your poetry offers and does and will do for so many souls in this world. May I share some of this magical poetry in my own personal poetry group Seema. My readers would be overjoyed to read your words,

Roopa Varma, Delhi, India (Feb 2016) -All of Seema's poems reflect a humane touch sprung from the heart especially her poems "A Father's Grief", and "All Trussed up, Packaged for delivery' which are soul stirring and real tear jerkers. The description of the kaleidoscopic view of her poems on nature is a delight because she brings the virtual nature before the eyes painted in all hues and shades. Juggling as a lady, daughter, sister, wife,mother,and career woman, she has beautifully woven threads of everyday life into simple verses and given a different twist to Romance, elevating the word "love" and consequent emotions to a new height for the readers. Her simple, yet realistic approach to the very basic everyday happenings which usually goes unnoticed in the hustle bustle and humdrum strikes a chord in each of us.'

Aneish Kumar, MD & Country Head, Bank Of Newyork Mellon, Mumbai (January 2016)

A versatile artist and poet of many hues besides leading one of the largest Banks The Bank Of New York Mellon as MD & Country Head, India - 'Close to my heart has always been works of great Poets of the past and current cuentury. I discovered that good poems can actually speak to us and make us think. And some of your poems did something similar to me. Your poems sometimes feel like song, they have a beat, some are more abstract and some mystical in a way but easily understood as literal writing.'

Akshat Shukla, Kanpur, India (December 2016) –

'Intricate imagery fabricated with subtlety of language; nuances of weather captured in a style that smacks of Imagism of the 20th century poets— the poem becomes a visual treat as words weave dramatic symbols.'

Kumarmani Mahakul (November 2015)

'Seema Jayaraman is Mumbai based Indian poetess of natural skills and gifted blessing who writes very wise, interesting and nice poems on life, nature and spiritual feelings. I notice that many of her poems are philosophical in nature and give amazing feeling on pleasant readings. Definitely she is one of the shining stars in the sky of literature to give glitter of light and gem of world poetic community. May God bring lots of happiness for her and her family. I wish her all the best for her continuous literary perseverance.'

2. A Father's Grief

John Kavanagh, UK I had a huge lump in my throat from listening to this in your voice, so sad and so inspirational at the same time, your skills are beyond even those of Shakespeare, and I do not offer this comment lightly but say it with my heart.

Charl Cilliers, Yzerfontein South Africa (11/8/2015) - You have a great heart of compassion, Seema

Stephani Kievaughan, USA (9/15/2015) – 'Beauty and honor and reverence and the chance to convey Compassion through empathy. Are these not the reason our Hearts and souls are not moved to write Poetry. I Submit it is a Noble way to express our regrets our hopes our passion to reminisce. We Dare to Look back committing the pangs of all which ails us deep down to be carved into stone with our own black tears as Ink upon the tips of our Quills.'

Geeta Radhakrishna Menon Mumbai, India (9/11/2015) - A tragic incident so powerfully portrayed! May God give courage and strength to the father to bear the irreparable loss.

Dear Seema, you have a compassionate heart and you have succeeded in evoking deep emotion in the readers.

Kelly Kurt Polo, USA (9/9/2015) - You poured out the raw emotion that most of us felt, especially parents. Words are not enough to describe the horror and inhumanity.

Valsa George Ernakulam, Kerala (9/9/2015) - We all have been shocked by the tragedy that befell on the Kurdi family in which a little boy Aylan and his brother with their mother got drowned, while fleeing from terror in an over crowded boat! Seema, you have so poignantly brought out the incident and expressed in powerful words your moral indignation over the spawning hatred growing between countries and the escalating violence in the name of religion and supremacy! I had to read and re read this many times to get the full impact and meaning of this stunning write!

3. **All Trussed Up, Packaged For Delivery (Against Human Trafficking)**

Mary Mc Creath (1/2/2016) - It is unbelievable that such things can happen in this day and age. I was very touched by your words. Such events need more exposure and to be written about to draw the attention of one and all to what is happening in our world. May this poem receive the exposure it needs to bring this event to the consciousness of many

Madathil Rajendran Nair (11/5/2015) - Gruesome. It is really gruesome. You shocked me out of my wits. May this not be true in a world where I pray every second all that I see and hear be just auspicious.

Sanjukta Nag (11/4/2015) - This poem has made me speechless. Such a heart breaking incident which proved again that only humans can be this much brutal. And still there is no end of it. You wrote it so intensely, as it leaves an impression on the heart of a reader. Very well knitted poem, beyond rating.

Akhtar Jawad (11/3/2015) - Although I am aware of the evil of human trafficking, but after reading this poem I was unmoved and shocked. The poetess has described the sad story in a heart touching manner. Man is still not better than a beast. A very impressive poem that makes us thinking about the cruelty.........................10

Valsa George (11/3/2015) - I am stupefied by the terror and horror of this wicked act which has surpassed the fraud and felony, we read in fiction! You have succeeded in communicating to the readers the monstrosity of this act! We wonder how man can be so beastly to do this to an innocent child, incapable of self defense. Man's mercenary interests lower him to the level of a beast!

Kelly Kurt (11/3/2015) - An important issue to rally against. I am always dismayed by the lengths people will go to for a profit. If only for a second they would see other people as fellow beings, perhaps even a loved one of their own and think how they would feel. Thank you, Seema

4. Why Blame Me, A Blood Moon

John Kavanagh, UK (6/03/2016) - I am now officially proclaiming that I am your number 1 fan Seema, this is the most beautiful way I have ever read and seen of the soul's way of seeing our universe. I don't have the words in my vocabulary to address the wholeness of this masterpiece of poetry. You are definitely gifted by those above us

What a difference when listened to in your own voice my dear Seema, you read it like you are a medium reading of the way beyond, your voice is enchanting, I closed my eyes and drifted on your every word, c, and I will truly at any opportunity share your wonderful words as far as I can reach in my part of the world, than you for your kindness in availing these soul sating poems that YOU have penned.

Ronnie Woodall (12/2/2015) - Very beautiful way to look at a blood moon! Two people can look at the same thing and see it in very different ways. Why not look for the light rather than dwell on the darkness? Seems like a good bargain to me. I enjoyed this romantic prose immensely!

Dorothy- A. Holmes (11/15/2015) - Thank you for this most special verse. An early morning treasure for me. A lesson in loveliness! Dorothy -A Poet Who Loves To Sing.

Loke Kok Yee (11/1/2015) - man is always blind to the beauty all around greed and power cover his eyes and treasures waiting are not found thanks for a lovely poem.

Bharati Nayak (10/18/2015) - This romantic vision of a celestial wedding – the red blush on Moon, s face with the closeness of the bride 'Earth' – against the backdrop of a 'Gandharva' marriage - is truly mesmerizing one. Thanks for sharing the wonderful poem.

Rajnish Manga (10/13/2015) - What a fantastic imagery and an equally profound narrative which is by far the most original idea on the subject. The arrangements and the setting for a Gandharva style of marriage has been perfectly visualised. All the customs, groom's and bride's fineries and the very special set of **emotions** reserved for this wedding day, are just matchless. This is a grand personification of a celestial happening par excellence. Do I still need to thank you for sharing a glittering spectacle with us, Seema ji?

Gangadharan Nair Pulingat (11/10/2015) - Fantastic. Like mixed jewels of different type in one ornament the words illumines as a clear like picture in sky

Jeri Martindale (11/10/2015) - Wonderful poem that takes us on a journey of the eclipse. We were unable to see it where I live due to thunderstorms that came through that night, however after reading your poem I now know exactly what it looks like. Lovely picture you painted!

Purnima Santhakumar -The earth, the moon and the sun- a very beautifully romantic visualization

Dr. Tony Brahmin (10/10/2015) - I selected these lines I liked in a separate sheet of paper first and then sat and thought about your genius. Wonderful my dear Poetess. Simply wonderful.

Oorimila Vijaykrishna Prahalad, Sydney, Australia - This meticulously crafted poem seems to encapsulate the cacophony of life and how thoughts and sentiments well up, wanting to break free but are lost in the din of everyday living. The poet beautifully sets the scene - runners pound on the tarmac (running perhaps being a metaphor for life itself) and thoughts struggle to surface up and find breathing space. "I can sneak my thoughts Aloud on cold unyielding tarmac To be trampled on by strangers." The harsh closing imagery leaves the reader with a sense of loss. The word 'trampled' driving home the point that they never stood a chance anyway.

5. Seattle Blossoms

Oorimila Vijaykrishna Prahalad, Sydney, Australia - The juxtaposition of contrasting worlds at many levels - the native land that the poet has left behind and the shores she works on, and the contrast between the natural world of the delicate cherry blossoms and the digital cosmos of her work. Beautifully expressed in this engaging poem.

Paul Reed, South Shields, UK (11/17/2015) - ...as I cross over the silently surging brook. What a powerful line with so many meanings.

Michael Walkerjohn, Heavensent, USA (9/20/2015) - The far between 'drawing kolams' and 'ISD calls'... painted prayers and onto subscriber dialing... similar, yet with so much difference... as is from beginning onto end... what a web of living, career and potential future... hard to imagine that this route is not a normal one... IAM happy that you have a moment to develop into phrase these looks in words into you daily thoughts and experiences... all of the best from this life, to you, and all of your relations... Michaelw1two

Roop Rekha Bhaskar, Dubai, UAE (9/5/2015) - Seema, i loved it! I saw myself in those lines, how accurately and wonderfully you have penned every detail. You made me see you, and the nature and your office too... And being far away from your home town creates such a slump sometimes. yet life goes on.

Stephani Kievaughan, USA (9/15/2015) - this was a delightful Wonderous testament of Your Sense of adventure and Wanderlust I Loved it all.

6. Rainbow Magik on Wall – Haiku

Charl Cilliers, South Africa (11/9/2015) - Love the images you subtlely use

Madathil Rajendran Nair (11/5/2015) - That is beautiful! A rainbow is has just visited me

Mary Mc Creath (10/13/2015) - You have a way with Haiku another delightful verse.

Purnima Santhakumar Coimbatore, India (10/5/2015) - Your crystals brought the rainbow home! !

Kumarmani Mahakul, Odisha, India (10/5/2015) - Amazing imagery is drawn here. Really wonderful sunrise drums the window. Interesting sharing....10

7. Monsoon Fury In March!!!

Anil Kumar Panda (10/2/2015) - You have woven a beautiful magic with rich vocabulary in this write, Awesome. Keep inking.

Ramesh T A Pondicherry, India (10/1/2015) - Monsoon fury is a magic that suddenly changes peaceful atmosphere sure!

Roop Rekha Bhaskar, Dubai, UAE (10/1/2015) - Charismatic write. Drops of water from the sky and a poetess to catch them in such picturesque phrase is delightful. This is a wonderful poem. (Report)

8. Her Sorrow

Roop Rekha Bhaskar (9/16/2015) -I am smitten with these lines. Sometimes the titles catch my eye. It is as enticing as the love that is hidden behind these lines

9. Mymmy Aaj Chutti Hai (Hindi Poem)

Akhtar Jawad, Pakistan (9/13/2015) - I am enchanted by the natural description in a typical Mumbai Bhsha. It's innocence, it's charms and it's effectiveness is amazing.

Gangadharan Nair Pulingat, Kerala (9/13/2015) - Little one's talent a pride and happiness that gives to the mother. The poet shared this to the members of poet's community and thanks for the same

10. My Loneliness

Stephani Kievaughan, USA (9/15/2015) - I think these verses are Seema declaring a thorough Comprehension of her hearts study on Empathy. A Love Comparable only to the Love That otherwise Only Comes From the many Hearts of God

Kumarmani Mahakul, Odisha, India (9/14/2015) - Loneliness speaks through expression of emotion and dates back to the year 1990. Really very interesting to read such an amazing poem which is well versed. Vision with dancing eyes holds splendor and laughter both here and the imagery speaks about strong message. A thoughtful and nice sharing

11. Time

Stephani Kievaughan, USA (9/15/2015) - 12 years old you say and you were pondering the trappings of time. Yes a wisdom of Lives gone past surely resides in the Soul of Such as You. Wisdom greater than the throngs of Humanity often spring forth from the spiritual wisdom of the Child. When their innocence dares with a boldness to speak the truth. never to be tamped down by the trappings of the society. Bound in their concrete sediment of Norms, and standards of their state of being trapped. likened unto a pebble in the oldest Concrete.

12. Dawn

Dr. Tony Brahmin, Dortmund, Germany (9/13/2015) This beautiful precious sight... it is the sense of beauty that is the foundation of poetic thinking. you had it very early in your life. let us thank God who is Beauty in itself. God gave you that great poetic gift. thank you. you emphasize the necessity to do hard work to achieve poetic heights. thank you

Valsa George, Kerala, India (9/9/2015) - Seema, I see that you were a full grown poet even at the age of twelve! You can easily add many more feathers to your cap! Greatly enjoyed this serene morning scene!

13. My Only Star

Stephani Kievaughan, USA (9/15/2015) - The verse's constantly beckoned me to understand your only favored and highly regarded star was such as a Black Hole you so brilliantly danced all around the subject matter without ever confessing nor declaring your favorite star was actually a Black Hole. Bravo Mrs. Jayaraman for such writings as these. I offer unto you a standing Ovation of praise. Clapping my hands in your General Direction and nodding out of respect. wearing a big Smile of pride for such as the Likes of you.

Valsa George, Kerala, India (9/9/2015) - It is an unseen brilliance, something mysterious hiding inside that gives shape and form to our thoughts and being! Let it come and radiate you that your songs rise like a crescendo! Beautiful, Seema!